Different Types of Depression

Characteristics and treatments

Depression Self-help Series – vol. 1

Joyce Zborower, M.A.

Contributing Author: John F. Walsh, M.S.

ISBN – 1495336441
ISBN-13 – 978-1495336447

D1620545

Table of Contents

Different Types of Depression

Characteristics and Treatments

Learning About Different Types of Depression

Types And Characteristics

Many people think that depression is just a feeling that affects behavior and mood. Depressed people aren't only experiencing psychological issues that can affect their moods or feelings; depression can lead to other issues such as medical problems or even death.

This is why people need to pay attention to the beginning signs of depression if they don't want to suffer from further problems. But not many people realize that there are different types of depression and each type has its own different symptoms.

What Is Depression
Most people will be experiencing up and downs during life. Sometimes they feel joyful and happy and sometimes they feel sad. Depression is generally associated with extreme feelings of sadness. It's often referred to as living in the darkness. They may feel useless, unworthy, and empty. They may feel as though life has no meaning and see themselves as pathetic and unworthy. They may experience anger whose source or reason they can't explain.

People should be aware if they start having these symptoms:

- They have uncontrollable negative feelings about themselves
- They sleep too much or they can't sleep at all
- They eat too much or they experience drastic loss of appetite which lead to drastic weight loss
- They feel worthless and useless
- They're easily irritated or upset
- They experience constant fatigue or listlessness
- They lose focus which can affect their performance at school or work
- Their mood swings (depression through elation) affect their relationships with other people

People experiencing such feelings need to consult a professional. Medical doctors are not usually educated in dealing with the effects of depression but can be useful in providing a referral to someone who can help.

When experiencing the above symptoms, it's best to consult a counselor, psychologist or psychiatrist who will be able to determine whether and what kind of special treatment is needed.

Types of Depression

There are three major types of depression:
1 -- Major Depression or Major Depressive Disorder:
Besides the general symptoms of depression common amongst depressed people, Major Depression is characterized by disabling symptoms that interfere with one's ability to function properly. A person may experience only one episode or she/he may have recurring episodes throughout their lifetime. Thoughts about suicide may be present and they often feel guilty for unknown reasons.

2 -- Dysthymia or Dysthymic Disorder.
This chronic disorder is characterized by constant depressive feelings that are not disabling but do keep the person from feeling good. The symptoms usually include a low level of self esteem and constant fatigue and low energy levels. It's not as severe as Major Depression, but it's the persistence of it that tends to be particularly troublesome.

3 -- Bipolar Disorder or Manic Depression.
As the name suggests, bipolar disorder consists of two phases that include depression and mania.

During the manic phase, a person can be very happy, very joyful and much energized; they can have such high peaks of elevated energy and mood that they tend to do dangerous things.

In the depression phase he/she can be very sad, very despondent. Feelings of worthlessness – uselessness – tend to occupy most of their thoughts . . . possibly even guilt feelings about inconsequential nothings. During this phase suicidal thoughts are common. All these feelings are accompanied by very low energy levels.

Other Types of Depression

In addition to these major depression types, there're also other different types of depression including:

-- SAD or Seasonal Affective Disorder
This kind of depression is affected and influenced mostly by seasons. It's most prevalent during winter months and can be alleviated with light therapy.

-- Postpartum Depression
It's a disorder that sometimes affects new moms after delivering their baby. Hormonal influences are believed to play a large part in this disorder so hormone replacement therapy is a common postpartum depression treatment.

-- Anxiety Depression
Social phobia or panic disorder is usually included in this type of depression.

-- Atypical Depression
This is a sub-type of Dysthymia or Major Depression.

-- Situational Depression
This type of depression is usually related to sudden changes or events, such as divorce, job loss, or relationship issue.

-- Chronic Depression
Chronic depression, as the name implies, can last for fully two years or more.

-- Double Depression
Patients are having two types of depression at once. For example, they may experience Major Depression and Dysthymia simultaneously.

-- Psychotic Depression

Delusions and hallucinations characterize this kind of behavior. It's very serious and can require medication and/or hospitalization in a mental health facility.

-- Melancholic Depression
The main symptom of this condition is that it is worse in the morning.

-- Catatonic Depression
Catatonia is characterized by an immobility of motor movements and behavior. It can be caused by emotional factors or physical adverse reactions to certain medications. There are various treatments available including benzodiazepine and ECT (electro convulsive therapy).

It's important to know which type of depression the patient is experiencing so they can get the right kinds of treatments to alleviate the disorder. Self-medication for these symptoms can lead to drug abuse and/or alcoholism. Seeking the assistance of qualified professionals such as a counselor, psychologist or psychiatrist is recommended. They will be able to determine whether medical treatments or behavioral therapies would be best to deal with these issues.

Finding out the exact depression types and the right treatments are important if people want to be free from these debilitating disorders.

References:
-
http://www.helpguide.org/mental/depression_signs_types_diagnosis_treatment.htm
- http://www.webmd.com/depression/guide/depression-types
- http://www.depression-help-resource.com/types-of-depression.htm

Free Online Tests for Depression

Geriatric Depression Scale – GDI

An "Am I Depressed?" Quiz for the Elderly

Bottom Line: The Geriatric Depression Scale (a self-reporting assessment tool) has been shown through statistically reliable research to be a suitable and relevant screening device to determine depression in the elderly. It is most accurate when administered to the elderly living independently within the community; less so with institutionalized individuals such as those living in nursing homes; and not suitable for use with dementia patients.

Originally developed in 1982 by J.Λ. Yesavage, et. al., the 30-question Geriatric Depression Scale to identify depression in the elderly has gone through some modification as well as some recent upgrades in availability. Some of those upgrades include the Scale being made available in various languages other than English.

Modification of the self-assessment tool came in 1986 with the introduction of the GDS Short Form, a 15-question screening tool that requires only 5 – 7 minutes to complete and can be self-administered or presented by a non-skilled assistant with minimal training in its use since, like the original, it requires only "yes" or "no" responses. Its ease of use makes it ideal for assessing ill patients as well as moderately cognitively impaired individuals.

The short form of this depression quiz was determined through research to be an adequate and reliable substitute for the original. All questions are meant to assess the patient's mood over the previous 7 day period. It is widely used in community settings, acute facilities and long-term care accommodations.

Availability of the GDS was greatly improved in 2011 with Mr. Yesavage's development of apps for viewing and taking the test on one's phone:
-- Click here to download the iPhone app from iTunes
-- Click here to download the Android app
For the elderly who are wondering, this depression checklist could help answer the question, "Am I depressed?"

How Is the Geriatric Depression Scale Scored

For the original 30-question assessment questionnaire:
0 – 10 = normal
11 – 19 = mildly depressive
20 – 30 = severely depressive

For the newer GDS Short Form:
0 – 4 = normal
5 – 8 = mild depression
9 – 11 = moderate depression
12 – 15 = severe depression

A word of caution here: The GDS is not a substitute for a complete psychological workup. To make a definitive diagnosis of clinical depression, GDS data should be considered in conjunction with other diagnostic criteria. Diagnoses should not be based solely on GDS responses.

Myth

It's common to think of depression as just a normal part of growing old. Life is winding down; there may be serious or chronic illnesses to deal with; children are grown and gone; once important goals may not have been achieved and time is running out. These and more are life situations that could lead to feelings of sadness or loneliness or depression. However, depression is not inevitable even if life is not all one had hoped for.

Depression is not a natural and normal part of aging.

It's important to find out if an older person feels depressed because, if left untreated, it can seriously affect their quality of life, their relationships, and their desire to keep keeping on. Depression is a potent risk factor in suicide.

According to a study done in 2004 by Juurlink, et. al., and reported in a journal article at http://nursingcenter.com, "older adults who died by suicide 'were almost twice as likely to have visited a physician in the week before the death' than were living control subjects." One can infer from this that they were looking for help – and didn't get it.

There is plenty of help for depression available if you know where to look. Your friendly family physician is not educationally equipped to deal with emotional issues. Their expertise is physical issues and, at best, may be able to provide a referral to a qualified counselor, psychologist or psychiatrist for emotional issues.

With proper and timely treatment, depression is often reversible to the point where the affected individual can live a more satisfying and enjoyable life.

References

-- http://www.public-health.uiowa.edu/icmha/outreach/documents/TheGeriatricDepressionScale.pdf

--
http://www.nursingcenter.com/library/journalarticle.asp?article_id=7
44981
-- http://en.wikipedia.org/wiki/Geriatric_Depression_Scale
-- http://www.medscape.com/viewarticle/447735

Beck Depression Inventory -- BDI-II

Depression Test for Adults Age 13 and Up

Bottom line: The Beck Depression Inventory (BDI, BDI-II) has proven itself to be a reliable and consistent assessment device for accurately separating depressed from non-depressed individuals 13-years-old and older – except for the elderly. *Recommendation:* may be used in research and/or clinical settings.

1996 saw the release of the latest version of the Beck Depression Inventory (BDI-II), a very widely used and respected 21-question, multiple choice, self-reporting depression check list for adults. The patient is asked to choose one of four possible responses that is most representative of their depressed condition. The choices are presented from mildest to severest and are given weighted scores. The higher the combined scores, the more depressed the individual is considered to be.

Originally developed by Dr. Aaron T. Beck to provide mental health professionals with a measure of the severity of depression in the subject, its primary use today is as a screening device to determine who is and who isn't depressed rather than as a diagnostic tool, but some professionals consider it accurate enough to provide quick diagnostic results.

Though Dr Beck's association with the development of the cognitive theory of depression is well known, the Beck Depression Inventory was created independently of that theory – or of any particular theoretical bias for that matter.

The BDI-II depression quiz is easy to administer and score, takes only about 5 minutes, and is exceptionally accurate. It provides insight into the patient's mood (how they're feeling about their situation of the previous two weeks) as well as how these feelings are affecting them physically (example: are they losing weight because they just don't have a desire to eat?).

The multiple choice answers are given weighted points of 0 to 3 corresponding to the severity of the patient's feelings then all the points are added together to provide a composite picture of the patient's overall state -- the higher the overall score, the greater the severity of the depression.

Cutoff designations for the depth of depression are:
0 – 13 = normal
14 – 19 = mild depression
20 – 28 = moderate depression
29 – 63 = severe depression
Patients within the severe depression group may well require hospitalization following a full psychological workup.

The BDI questionnaire is currently online here.

TEENS -- Since the bottom cut-off age is 13, the BDi-II can be successfully used as an online teenage depression test.

ELDERLY -- Sharp and Lipsky (2002), as reported in a paper published by musc.edu, found the BDI psychometric data for elderly patients to be mixed (i.e. not clear cut as with younger adults) and suggested "the BDI may not be the best screening measure for elderly patients"[1]. For assessing depression in the elderly, the Geriatric Depression Scale is a better option.

References

1.-- http://www.musc.edu/dfm/RCMAR/Beck.html
-- http://en.wikipedia.org/wiki/Beck_Depression_Inventory
-- http://www.pearsonassessments.com/HAIWEB/Cultures/en-us/Productdetail.htm?Pid=015-8018-370
-- http://cps.nova.edu/~cpphelp/BDI.html

Edinburgh Postpartum Depression Scale – EPDS

Depression Test for Pregnant Women and New Moms

CAUTION: "The Edinburgh Postnatal Depression Scale is only a screening tool and does not diagnose postpartum depression. If you get high scores on the scale, it indicates a need for more thorough evaluation that must be done by appropriately licensed health care professionals."1

Bottom line: The EPDS, developed in Scotland in 1987 to assist doctors in identifying postpartum depression (PPD) in new mothers, has proven to be a valid and reliable screening tool for that purpose. It is also valid for use with pregnant women prior to delivery.

The EPDS is a 10-item questionnaire that is quick and easy to administer, easy to score, and easy to understand. As with other depression scales, the questions are geared to assess current mood – guilt feelings, suicidal thoughts, etc. -- (past 7 days as opposed to 2 weeks in the other scales) as well as physical symptoms of clinical depression – sleep disturbance, low energy, etc.

Other signs of depression might include crying, feeling miserable, being unable to laugh, negative self-talk, feeling anxious for no apparent reason, thinking about suicide.

Why Test for Postpartum Depression?

According to various studies, PPD in new mothers may be as high as 13 - 20% with many cases remaining undiagnosed and, therefore, untreated. Left untreated, PPD affects the mother/child relationship and may contribute to life-long adverse effects for all involved.

In the more serious cases, the mother may even plan to harm the child or herself.

Another major reason to screen for postpartum depression is to give businesses the opportunity to design strategies that reduce PPD within their workforce.

Health care costs for women with PPD are higher than for those who do not experience this condition. According to psychcentral.com, "depression among workers has been shown to cost U.S. employers $44 billion (with a B) per year in lost productivity and about $12.4 billion in health care expenditures. . . .Employed women are more likely to experience postpartum depression if they have lower job flexibility, lower social support, and higher total workload."[2]

Such strategies might include:
1 – designing policies that promote childbirth recovery and successful return to work

2 – having key personnel collaborate with top human resources personnel to support those policies which ease the transition for working mothers

3 – provide insurance policies that are mental health services friendly.

There are several websites that offer online tests for postpartum depression. Since the test is the same on all websites, you can access one of them by clicking here.

References

1.-- http://www.psymed.info/default.aspx?m=Test&id=71&l=3
2.-- http://psychcentral.com/news/2012/04/10/postpartum-depression-linked-to-higher-health-care-costs/36891.html
--
http://en.wikipedia.org/wiki/Edinburgh_Postnatal_Depression_Scale

Characteristics of Depression

"What Does Depression Feel Like?"

by guest author: John F Walsh, M.S.

"I don't like standing near the edge of a platform when an express train is passing through. I like to stand right back and if possible get a pillar between me and the train. I don't like to stand by the side of a ship and look down into the water. A second's action would end everything. A few drops of desperation." - Winston Churchill (1874-1965)

(Names and places have been changed to protect privacy.)

In everyone's life there are periods of "what's the use"? But clouds recede and optimism returns ... for most people. I'd like to introduce you to three of my clients. Two are dealing with the consequences of depression and one has a different agenda.

Diana works for the telephone company manning the computer. She has two sisters and two brothers. Her father is a lineman in North Carolina. Her mother and the other sons and daughters live in Palm Beach County, Florida. Diana lives in Charlotte. NC. She has a boyfriend whom she is afraid of. She smokes marijuana and has been known to take pills.

Don is in his late 20's. My major contact with him is when he is brought into the emergency room following self inflicted knife wounds. He is a single child not much is known about his parents as he lives alone. These episodes seem to occur about once every two months. When these events happen he is usually accompanied by a different distraught girlfriend. Don is unemployed.

Bob is a master's chess player. He lives with his family. He is well spoken, conservatively dressed and in his second year of college. He is not currently in a relationship. He feels like an outcast on occasion as his interest in classical music, especially chamber music, is not shared by his peers. On occasion he works with his father's catering service but has little interest in following this line of work.

I received an emergency phone call that Diana was freaking out. I went to the second floor apartment she shared with her girlfriend. There were two girls and four guys smoking opiated hash with discordant music blasting. Everyone in the living room seemed oblivious to any emergency, and pretty much oblivious to anything but the hash, in my opinion.

The girl friend who made the call ushered me into the bedroom where Diana was having a meltdown. Feeling that Johnny Rotten and the Sex Pistols did not contribute to a calm ambiance I was seeking so I shouted to shut the damn thing off. I might have had better luck discussing proportional representation with a herd of grazing cattle, so I just pulled the cord out of the wall. Diana was shivering, sitting on the floor with her arms hugging her knees. She was aware of me being there and seemed mortified that I saw her in this condition. I helped her up and we left the apartment. Approaching the stairs Diana exploded into resistance causing us both to tumble down the concrete steps. I shielded her head from making contact. I admitted her to the psychiatric wing of the local hospital.

Another emergency call from a hysterical woman. Don had set himself on fire and was sitting in his car in the hospital parking lot. The fire department had arrived and Don had received minor burns to his chest and arms. There was an added issue. Apparently there was a bomb in the trunk of the car. That involved the local police and representatives from Shaw Air Force Base Bomb Squad. Standing around the hospital parking lot waiting for the bomb to go off was the hospital administer, three firemen, four cops, myself and a screaming girlfriend.

The bomb experts from Shaw asked who was in charge? "Well that kinda depends on just which level of authority you might consider", I thought to myself and pointed to the senior police officer. The bomb squad elected to drive the car back to Shaw, the firemen folded their hoses and left, the cops left leaving one to fill out the incident report. The hospital administer was relieved that a bomb didn't go off in the hospital parking lot, the girl had now stopped screaming and Don was back on the psych unit.

Bob was having a bad day. He had been up three nights straight, wouldn't eat and kept perseverating on Kasparov pawn B-5. He got into the family car and drove off and it wasn't until 14 hours later that he was located at a truck stop 300 miles away, crying. He was admitted to a local hospital, given a sedative and kept under observation.

Diana looked out the meshed screened fourth floor window at a girl getting into her automobile and thought to herself, "I really am crazy!" She was taken for a series of twelve electro shock treatments (EST). She described her experience following her first day back to work.

"It was weird. I would open a drawer and see a sweater. It had to be mine but I've never seen it before. At work I had a little trouble remembering which floor my office was located. Kathy a co-worker greeted me. I know she has children but I can't remember their names. It's like you have to concentrate so hard putting the pieces together you don't have time to feel depressed."

Don had little recollection of what happened. Because every time we are called he is so slobbering drunk that we could never get any useful information about him. Even in moments of rare sobriety his answers were vague and incoherent. He did recognize me and regarded me in a positive light. His chest and arms had so many cut scars that he looked like an AAA road map. It was his twelfth hospital admission.

Bob had been noncompliant with his bi-polar medication. He explained, "It's like everything was so clear I understood everything." I asked him what Kasparov pawn B-5 was about. He explained that in Kasparov vs. Topalov, 1999 one of the most outstanding chess matches ever, the move of the pawn to B-5 was Kasparov's first defensive move that shaped the rest of the game. As for why he refused to take the medication that would treat his condition he explained that when he was hyper it was like the world was in Technicolor, that people around him were moving and thinking in molasses. When he takes the medication it feels like he was dropped down an elevator shaft back into a black and white world. I wish they made a medication that let you down slower and more gentle.

Any thoughts as to the appropriate diagnosis for the three? Let's hop forwards a few years.

Diana is now living in Palm Beach, Florida with a musician who plays for the Boston Pops.
They have a young daughter. Diana is off medication. She feels more complete.

Bob is still living with his parent. His episodes are less severe and further apart.

I received a telephone call from the Sheriff of Union County wondering if I had ever come across a Don XXX. He was scheduled for trial on 7 counts of burglary and one assault. Problem was that every time he's due in court he's always in the hospital.

A solution was reached. Don stood trial and was sentenced to 8-12 years. That was the last emergency call we received regarding Don. It helps when agencies work more closely together.

Depression During Pregnancy

Signs -- Symptoms – Consequences

Depression during pregnancy can occur prior to delivery or after delivery. Anti-partum depression, the technical name for depression before delivery, often starts on the forth month of pregnancy and becomes more intense during the eighth month. Postpartum depression, depression after delivery, can begin as early as the second week following delivery or up to six or eight months following delivery.

If postpartum depression is a mild form of 'baby blues', it often subsides on its own. If, however, the symptoms are severe or persist for a very long time, professional intervention by a qualified counselor, psychologist, or psychiatrist may be required.

Over 12 per cent of women suffer from depression during pregnancy though most cases are left unattended because the symptoms are often mistaken for common hormonal imbalances experienced by women when carrying a child.

Signs of Depression During Pregnancy

Depression is a mental disorder that affects the normal functioning of the brain, the body and hormones. In pregnant women, normal hormone imbalances caused by the pregnancy are thought to be the leading cause of this condition. Whether it occurs during pregnancy or after delivery, the symptoms are the same.

Here is a sampling of the physical symptoms of depression:

• Insomnia
• Oversleeping
• Sadness

- Crying
- Social isolation
- Anxiety
- Hopelessness
- Suicidal thoughts
- Self guilt
- Loss of appetite
- Overeating

Risk Factors

Most women do not experience depression during pregnancy. Some of the factors that trigger ante-partum depression include:

- Previous depression attacks
- Childhood maltreatment
- More than three previous births
- Single motherhood
- Lack of social support
- Cigarette smoking
- Young mothers especially those below 20 years
- Low family income
- Domestic violence and marital constraints
- Fertility treatments prior to conception
- Previous miscarriage
- Life events
- Unplanned pregnancy
- Pregnancy complications
- History of PMS

Consequences of Ante-partum Depression

Women who experience depression for more than two consecutive weeks often try to counter their low moods by:

- Use of tobacco products leading to major complications
- Use of alcohol and other substances
- Suicide attempts and suicide deaths
- Starvation

• Failure to go for prenatal care

These practices also have a deleterious effect on the developing fetus resulting in:

• Infant temperament being affected with the child developing mood swings with age
• Childhood behavior being affected with children becoming bullies
• Fetal growth is also affected with many children experiencing stunted growth
• Miscarriage and/or low baby weight
• Postpartum depression -- 25% of all cases of postpartum depression are attributed to ante-partum depression

Baby blues is the milder form of postpartum depression and affects 50 per cent of first time mothers. Its symptoms resemble those of ante-partum depression and tend to subside without intervention by the eighth month after delivery. This form of depression often leads to relationship problems between the mother and the child, other children and even between partners.

Management of Depression During Pregnancy

Exercise, proper nutrition and adequate rest are some of the strategies you can use to relieve the symptoms of depression. Pregnant women are encouraged to get enough exercise and rest in order to manage their moods and prevent the development of chronic depression. Chronic or severe depression requires the intervention of a qualified professional.

Psychotherapy is one of the popular treatments for depression. The patient is thoroughly interviewed to determine all the risk factors involved then an appropriate therapy and perhaps some medication is prescribed.

The mental health practitioner works hand in hand with the obstetrician to determine the best antidepressant for the patient. This is because antidepressants may have adverse effects on the unborn baby and can even lead to congenital malfunctions. Other maternal complications such as gestational diabetes may also be triggered by the use of antidepressant therapy.

It is important while pregnant to watch out for the physical symptoms of depression and take the most appropriate actions in order to prevent further complications for the mother as well as the child.

References

The New England Journal of Medicine: Depression during Pregnancy
URL: http://www.nejm.org/doi/full/10.1056/NEJMcp1102730

American Pregnancy Association: Depression during pregnancy
URL:
http://www.americanpregnancy.org/pregnancyhealth/depressionduri ngpregnancy.html

USNews: Coping with depression during pregnancy
URL: http://health.usnews.com/health-news/family-health/articles/2008/10/23/coping-with-depression-during-pregnancy

Harvard Medical School: Depression during pregnancy and after
URL:
http://www.health.harvard.edu/newsweek/Depression_during_pregn ancy_and_after_0405.htm

Thought Disorder

Thought Disorder in a Bipolar Client's Mind
a case study by guest author: John F. Walsh, M.S.

Saul is a 28 year old single white male who lives with his parents in a nice suburban Tudor styled home. His onset occurred when he was a sophomore in a private college. He has had three hospitalizations.

(*Note:* I met Saul … not his real name … at a computer club. When he learned I was a psychologist he began to sound me out. After awhile he felt comfortable letting me into his perceptions about having a Bi-polar disorder. This is from memory how he shared his insight with me.)

∧∧∧∧∧∧∧∧∧∧∧∧∧∧∧∧∧∧∧∧∧∧∧∧∧∧∧∧∧

"My name is Saul. I play chess and I'm good at it. I'm ranked as a master. I'm also diagnosed with a disease called Bi-polar. This means there are times when my brain is faster than my body. To be honest, I like the feeling. Hyper means never having to say, you're Saully.

Sorry, I get that way. Language becomes a toy to play with rather than just a way to communicate. But it does bug me that you can have cancer and you only have cancer. But with me I don't just have bipolar I am bipolar I reject that. There are times when I get despondent but its more likely I feel excitement and the people around me just seem stupid. They say I'm non compliant. I'm naughty. I don't behave. I need my medication they say.

Let me tell you why I don't like to take medicine. When I'm high I feel like everything is explained. That I understand things at the molecular level. My surroundings are in technicolor.

When I get a shot or take the pill my world turns from color to black and white, and I feel like I fell down an elevator shaft. If they would only make a pill that would ease my decompression more slowly.

I do see, I guess, what other people seem to see. When I'm manic the way I talk there are times I talk too fast and stumble over words. I understand what I want to say but my mouth seems unable to shape the words and people say I'm talking too loud. But people are too damn slow and it pisses me off.

That's why I like chess, you can't just jump around like you can in checkers, you have to see the boulevard and the alleyways before you make your decision to move.
Shatranj it was called and they never said "Check mate" it was "Shah Mat". Means "Death to the Shah" in Farsi.

But, you're not a chess player, I can tell. You want to know what it feels like to be bi-polar and why "I'm non compliant. "Compliant amenable, biddable, obedient, conformable, docile, law-abiding, submissive, tractable". Do I appear docile or submissive to you?

I do take the medicine but it is like what I said before I don't like taking a drug that defines me as being crazy and no matter how you gloss it over that's what it is.

When I feel fine I want to feel more fine and that's when I get into trouble. Because it's a fight. I don't like a drug that controls how I feel. "I know you feel happy but its not the kind of happy that we have prescribed for you." But if I don't comply I wind up in the hospital, and people know I'm crazy.

But I've learned to live with it. Yet while I know I'm intelligent I'm basically shy around people and not very trusting. Having mental problems will do that to you.

Controlling Situations

**Recognizing Manipulative People and Controlling Situations
EXCLUSIVE:**
An excerpt from Clinical Psychology – A Professional Perspective
– memoirs and experiences -- a book by guest author: John F.
Walsh, M.A.

It's my observation that when you first meet a new acquaintance
there is a period of ambivalence. You present your social face as
welcoming but assessing whether to trust this new person in your
life. If you like what you see you show your good cards hoping to
make a good impression. If not you make whatever excuse you favor
to put distance between the two of you. In this article we'll look at
what it feels like to deal with manipulative people in controlling
situations.
If the relationship deepens there can be resistance to letting down an
inner wall, again protecting the "ME" from hurt or betrayal or
simply from not wanting to expose yourself that quickly in your
relationship.

For whatever reason, your emotions allow you to lower the
drawbridge to your private face. When that happens there is a warm
ebb and flow of personal information exchanged and the feeling that
the two of you are now one in spirit.

Of course there is always the neurotic me. It even happens among
therapists.

Mary was a social worker in a clinic I worked at in North Carolina.
She was a woman in her 40's who had a series of bad marriages. She
was a kind Earth Mother who would occasionally show up at work
with a black eye or new bruise. One time she didn't show for work
for a week taking sick time. She claimed that she tripped and fell
down the cellar stairs. That week she filed for divorce.

Six months later she was in love again, a man with a cute nickname, "Hacksaw". She brought him around to meet us. The guy might as well have had a spitting cobra tattooed on his face with a scar running down one cheek and over to the next guy. BAD NEWS. But she was happy.

Some people, I fear, put too much oil on their drawbridge. I think that sociopaths seem to have built-in radar that detects the vibrations of an easy and vulnerable mark.

Neurotics need do well enough on their own and don't need the assistance of a sociopath.

Men or women who feel depressed and down on themselves can be a green light to an exploitative sociopath who poses as a rescuing savior.

Let me give two examples of how such a man can spoil the day of a depressed woman or, to be realistic about it, any woman.
Let's posit two manipulative approaches, the way of the wolf and the way of the fox.

The wolf is more primal and like their cousins of the sea, the shark, their approach is primal.

To illustrate, one of my acquaintances is a young girl 18 years of age. Her brother and her father are both members of the Canadian Royal Mounted Police.

Our wolf is unaware of that fact and dates the girl. He comes across as a diamond in the rough with a nice smile and a bit of a bad boy image. Problem is it's not an image, he is aggressive and demanding and what he demands is that she puts out for him which she resists. She successfully fights him off at a cost of a broken arm and three ribs.

He runs away and she is torn between telling her family and risk being told that she must have done something to lead him on like the way she dresses and flirts -- which is a stupid argument. If she drove a beautiful convertible could we say that her sexy car justified an auto theft?

While in the hospital, even though she feels guilty she does tell her family.

The wolf is caught. At the trial his attorney knows not to elect trial by jury, and tells him not to open his mouth. At sentencing our wolf feels justified in explaining his reasonableness. His rationale . . . ? "If she hadn't fought so much I wouldn't have had to hurt her".

Sometimes they just make it easy instead of the agreed four years the judge gave him the max eight years.

Then there are the Foxes. These guys are great at seduction. They will say exactly what you want to hear. They will curry and preen your ego and once they catch you turning starry eyes they will start tearing you down, messing with your head and educating you to the fiction that your opinions are naive and only their outlook is valid. Foxes will totally convince you that their farts are a privilege granted. While our fox maybe not legally sociopathic in my mind they are abusive to the soul.

The key to masculine management is to be alert to your chi. In other words if you go into a room with him and you leave feeling refreshed, alive, valued and confident, then your chi is positive.

On the other hand if you go into a mental space with him and when you leave you feel depressed, insecure, intimidated, confused and worthless, if you did not bring those emotions INTO the room, then you have been manipulated (or outfoxed, if you will).

Manipulation is defined as exerting shrewd or devious influence especially for one's own advantage. The term has something of a negative connotation but it is what it is -- neither good nor bad. It just is.

When you are faced with the television commercial of a giant digitized cheeseburger with one bite taken out of it shoved in your face and your salivary glands springs into Pavlovian response or when you see a sleep aid commercial with beautiful blue butterflies fanning you asleep while cute little chipmunks cheerfully pull the blanket up to your chin, you've been professionally manipulated.

I construct three types of interactive manipulations:
-- Manipulation of behavior – trying to get you to do what I want you to do.
-- Manipulation of emotions – trying to get you to feel the way I want you to feel.
-- Manipulation of the situation - trying to change the dynamics of the situation.

Manipulation of behavior can work as long as no one catches you at it. Say you are a pretty girl in white gloves who gets a flat tire. You don't want to get hot and sweaty so you stand by the tire, jack in hand, looking confused and helpless. A car pulls up and you say. "The round rubber thingie got all smooshed and I don't know what to do."

The driver smiles and says, "I know you, you're Crash Corrugate. I saw you racing at the Daytona Speedway last Sunday. Rumor has it that you can change a tire in one minute and three seconds."

Caught! Best thing to do is smile, admit that you really could use the help and appeal to his better nature.

Manipulation of emotions is usually unfair and counter-productive. Again we take our above-mentioned girl who wakes up filled with energy and ready to jog through the park on such a fine morning. She comes down the stairs and there sits her mother in the one spot of the house where avoiding her is impossible.

Her mother gives a weary but heartfelt sigh.

"Mother, what's wrong"?

"Nothing, dear. Have a good time. Don't worry about me"?

There were probably many things the girl had on her agenda, jogging through the park, checking the new sales, even pricing the new car she had her eye on. Worrying about Mom just didn't make the list. But then she feels a pang of guilt. Then she feels anger for feeling guilty and guilty for feeling anger -- after all, "Mother almost died giving birth to you." She has been telling you that on a regular basis whenever she feels her wishes slighted.

Manipulation of emotions: I saw a young fellow who had been dating a girl he was obsessed with. She broke off the relationship because in her mind he was too needy.

His rejoinder to keep her affection? "My brother died. My family hates me. You can't leave. You're all I've got!" This romantic declaration was as welcome as a gift of a dead mackerel on her lap.

If in your relations with a person, you go into a room with a positive feeling but leave with negative guilt or angry feelings, you may have been manipulated emotionally. Conversely, if every other day you feel angry, offended, betrayed and that others are being unfair, then you may need to see if you are not emotionally manipulating others.

Manipulation of the situation: Here you are trying to influence an outcome. This is often called having a "strategy". A football coach devising a playbook to outwit the opposition, or a politician negotiating a compromise are manipulations of the situation. On a more personal level, planning a surprise party is the same kind of strategy. This is probably the fairest form of manipulation.

So, when you are offered that giant digitized cheeseburger with one bite taken out of it shoved in your face and your salivary glands springs into Pavlovian response, will you bite the cheeseburger or will the cheeseburger bite you?

End of Excerpt

Multiple Personality Disorder

Fact Or Fiction?
By guest author: John F. Walsh, M.S.

Albert Hunsticker, during his day, was President of the Illinois Psychological Association. He had an advance degree that exceeded the Ph.D. He was a Diplomate in Clinical psychology. In fact he was on the Board of Examiners for the Diplomate degree. At this level of expertise one would expect the parting of the seas at Galilee or lifting tall buildings with a flicker of thought to be child's play. I was fortunate to have him as a teacher.

One day, six years after the movie "Three Faces of Eve" hit the theaters the subject of Multiple Personality Disorders was brought up in class. Dr. Hunsticker was asked his opinion. With a self deprecating chuckle said, "If in your career you come up with a multiple personality disorder, consider yourself very fortunate and be sure to write a book. Should you come up with two in your career then you have misdiagnosed both of them."

That was 1963. Since then Cris Sizemore (the woman whom the movie was based upon) has had a total of 20 "faces" and has gone on the lecture circuit. I have attended one of her appearances. Multiple Personality Disorder is now called Dissociative Disorder.

However a number of controversies surround dissociative disorder in adults as well as children. First, there is ongoing debate surrounding the etiology of dissociative identity disorder (DID), commonly referred to as multiple personalities. The crux of this debate centers on whether or not DID is the result of childhood trauma or iatrogenesis. Iatrogenesis is defined as "Induced in a patient by a physician's activity, manner, or therapy." (Score one for Dr. Hunsticker).

The Mayo Clinic http://www.mayoclinic.com/health/dissociative-disorders/DS00574 approaches this controversy stating:

"We all get lost in a good book or movie. But someone with dissociative disorder escapes reality in ways that are involuntary and unhealthy. The symptoms of dissociative disorders — ranging from amnesia to alternate identities — usually develop as a reaction to trauma and help keep difficult memories at bay."

One of my clients was raped by a black man. This was the South before Roe v. Wade. The procedure was for two clinicians a psychologist and an MD. come to an agreement that an abortion was justified. The administrator of the clinic was new so he refused to allow an abortion to occur. This left me with a "where do we go from here" situation.

My client came in for a medication appointment which was difficult as she was in her third trimester. I greeted her and saw that she was very agitated. With an abdomen that had the shape of a watermelon she claimed "Oh, I'm not pregnant, that's my sister, she's the one whose pregnant."

So what is this, Pre partum depression?

Post traumatic stress disorder is also associated with depression and dissociative disorders.

Dr. Matthew Tull is an associate professor and director of anxiety disorders research in the Department of Psychiatry and Human Behavior at the University of Mississippi Medical Center in Jackson contends; "There are several types of dissociative disorders, all of which cause a change in consciousness, memory, identity, or how one views his or her surroundings. This change can come on abruptly or slowly, and it may not happen all the time."

The DSM-IV (Diagnostic and Statistical Manual Forth edition) includes 5 types of dissociative disorders: One of the five is: "Dissociative Identity Disorder: This disorder used to be called, "Multiple Personality Disorder." A person with dissociative identity disorder will have two or more separate identities that each have their own way of thinking and relating to the world. To have this disorder, a minimum of two of these identities must also take control over the person's behavior again and again. Finally, the person with dissociative identity disorder may also have difficulty remembering personal information that, like dissociative amnesia, goes beyond simple forgetfulness."

So what is real and what is chimera? As Fox news is fond of saying, "We report and you decide."

Suicidal Thoughts

Suicidal Thoughts and Suicide Decisions
by guest author: John F. Walsh, M.S.

HELP RESOURCES
VA Suicide Hotline: 1-800-273-TALK (8255)

National Suicide Hotline: 1-800-SUICIDE (784-2433)

"It's not that I really want to die, it's just that I will trade it just to be free of the pain I feel."

"I can't face things going right for me, it always turns out bad".

"But that the dread of something after death,
The undiscovered country, from where no traveler
returns, puzzles the will, And makes us rather bear
those ills we have Than fly to others that we know not of?
Thus conscience does make cowards of us all,"
Hamlet

Thoughts of ending your life can be as fleeting as looking down from a tall building and having that flash of thought that makes you back away from the edge. Or it can be sustained such as the feeling that you don't belong and the animosity of your peers seeds rejection and shame.

Tormented thoughts of suicide have plagued Men and Women throughout the ages.

As for successful attempts, the American Association of Suicidology reports that suicide in 2007 was the tenth leading cause of death in the US, accounting for 34,598 deaths. The overall rate was 11.3 suicide deaths per 100,000 people. An estimated 11 attempted suicides occur per every suicide death. And those are the reported attempts for America.1 In fact, as world economies worsen suicide rates in countries around the world are going up.

There is another source of suicides reported that our government would rather you not know. "Since 9/11, more military personnel and veterans have committed suicide than the total dead from both wars in Iraq and Afghanistan combined (total Americans killed in wars = 6,200)3, and this tragedy is occurring despite the best of intentions and programs offered by the Departments of Defense and Veterans Affairs. . . . Still worse is a Centers for Disease Control estimate that 18 veterans from all wars commit suicide every day — that's 6,500 a year!"2 That's a total of around 55,000 vets that have committed suicide since 9/11 . . . a totally shocking number! Our success in teaching young boys to kill is making some finding it hard to live.

Estimates of post-traumatic stress disorder and traumatic brain injury vary widely, but a ballpark figure is that the problems afflict at least one in five veterans from Afghanistan. One study found that by their third or fourth tours in Iraq or Afghanistan, more than one-quarter of soldiers had such mental health problems.

Preliminary figures suggest that being a veteran now roughly doubles one's risk of suicide. For young men ages 17 to 24, being a veteran almost quadruples the risk of suicide, according to a study in The American Journal of Public Health.

An example is a client I treated. Let's call him Joe.

Joe is a former Navy Seal. (SEa Air Land). He is an expert in killing "the enemy". His team saw combat on the Afghan-Pakistan border. On one mission the Intel was totally wrong. They did a HALO jump but landed in a hot zone. They had to fight their way to a landing zone and to safety, but the destination was compromised and when they reached the coordinates they came under mortar fire.

Joe saw a figure attempt to throw a grenade. He rolled and open fire, killing his opponent. It was then he realized he had just murdered a 17 year old girl. What he thought was a grenade was in reality a beanbag.

Attempting to reach the escape helicopter, he was hit in the stomach by a mortar fragment and spent three months in a hospital. He was discharged, but the pictures of the event were seared into his thoughts. He felt the only occupation he was trained for was killing another human being.

When I saw him he was in the throws of PTSD (Post traumatic stress disorder). He was harassing a girl who he heard had a congenital heart disease. He was begging her to take his living heart. It frightened her.

Joe was strong in his belief that he was a murderer and his only salvation was to die in the service of another. He took a job driving an ambulance. His co-workers admired him but didn't want to ride with him. ("Son-of-a-bitch will do crazy shit!"). Movie stunts don't translate well in real life. When I saw him he couldn't sleep and was plagued with flashback. While others saw him as a hero in service for his country, he could only see himself a murderer.

I worked with him for about four months. He still drives like a maniac but at least he is focused on future goals.

Working emergency services including after hours emergency on call I would estimate about 40% are a credible suicide risk. In the time I worked there I did lose one.

The telephone call came in about 9:30pm on a Saturday night. It was a woman who felt her husband was suicidal. When asked for clarification she said that he was drunk and wouldn't stop cleaning his gun. I asked if she tried talking to him and perhaps take possession of the weapon. She elected not to do that. I told her to either take him to the ER or call the police to escort him and I would have the paperwork (for emergency evaluation) ready.

The lethality of the situation speaks to impulsive acting out. He was drunk and he had a gun in his hand. We routinely do not call the police ourselves as there is no way we can assess the lethality of the situation. I received no follow up call from her which was not unusual.

It was Monday before I found out that he killed himself.

Apparently the wife had decided the best option was to gather the children and drive to the church to pray for his soul. While they were at church he shot himself.

While I acknowledge the power of prayer, there is something to be said for the power of common sense.

There is a belief that suicides occur when the victim senses that the family wants to be rid of them. That message seems to have been sent in this case.

My involvement with the police brought me to confront suicides attempts sometimes ongoing and sometimes postmortem.

I was riding with a unit in Charlotte, North Carolina when we received a 10-56 call in a middle class neighborhood. Apparently a white male 37 years of age, divorced, was at his mother-in-law's house with his three children. He was intoxicated and in his bathrobe. The woman had addressed him stating that he needed to get himself together, to stop drinking and go out and find a job. The woman reported that he smiled and replied, "Nah, I'd rather do this." He pulled a revolver and shot himself in the left temple killing himself.

When we arrived we found the children hysterical being comforted rather unsuccessfully by the mother-in-law. The victim was laying on the carpet partially on his left side. The force of the blow-back of the weapon's discharge resulted in fragments of the victim's tongue protruding from the exit wound. Kind of messed his profile.

In my book, Clinical Psychology – A Professional Perspective – memoirs and experiences, I describe another facet of an impulse attempt:

"About an hour later we received a call from the EMT that a suicide was in progress but the person was refusing treatment. We rolled up; the ambulance was in the driveway its emergency lights painting red swaths on the white wood. Inside was an angry mother, two EMT personnel and a paunchy looking white male in his twenties holding a knife. He had deeply cut his left forearm, blood was streaming so he had cut a vein. Had it been an artery it would have been spurting.

Legally a person has the right to refuse treatment. He was over 21 so his mother couldn't sign papers on him. The blood pooled on the floor as we waited. Most people freak when they see blood. As a point of information loss of blood becomes critical when enough blood is lost that a bath towel becomes saturated.

Snooping a bit I found a handwritten card on the mantle. It was a scribbled note to the boy's father saying that the father was right . . . he was a complete waste and he decided not to bother the family with his presence.

The boy finally fell down unconscious from the blood loss. This was what we were waiting for. He was now in a state of diminished consciousness so not able to make decisions in his own best interest. I nodded and the EMT went to work, packing him up and injecting a saline solution in his arm and transporting him to the ER."

Women don't like guns. As a rule they are more apt to take pills. When a person takes three or five pills I see it as less a suicide and more a cry for attention. Ten or twenty pills they are really trying to check out.

I'm familiar with an actress who depended upon her beauty since she was a child actress. She couldn't face becoming old so she set the stage. She lit candles and put on her favorite sheets and her flowing nightgown. Having established a beautiful memory picture she took a handful of pills.

It didn't go quite as planned. Twenty five minutes later her body is expelling the pills from both ends of her body. She staggered to the bathroom slipped on her vomit and hit the commode with her front teeth and drowned in her own vomit. The National Enquirer has the photo.

I tell this story when I get a client enchanted with the fantasy of a picturesque death.

To me suicide is self murder. If I'm involved I care little about the reason. Kill yourself on your own time not mine.

There are things I look for in a person who is thinking of suicide.

Is the person having trouble concentrating or thinking clearly? Have they set up a situation conducive to impulsive acting out behavior such as standing on a ledge, performing self-destructive behaviors, such as heavily drinking alcohol, using illegal drugs, or cutting their body?

By contrast is the person creating an organized attempt such as giving away belongings or talking about going away or the need to "get my affairs in order."Are they giving a signal that they are retreating from social interacting such as losing interest in activities that they used to enjoy? A sudden change of behavior, especially calmness after a period of anxiety, losing interest in activities that they used to enjoy, pulling away from friends or not wanting to go out. Talking about death or suicide, or even saying that they want to hurt themselves, feeling hopeless or guilty, major change in sleep or eating habits, talking about feeling hopeless or guilty are all strong warning signs of an attempted suicide.

While you might think that killing yourself is relatively easy. I had a girl who had a surefire attempt, in more ways than one. She took off her clothes and sat in the bathtub so as to contain the mess. She placed a double barreled shotgun to her abdomen and pulled both barrels. She lived. But not without a lot of internal damage that in no uncertain terms she had to live with.

When I'm on the phone and I don't know the person or his or her intent. I listen for any clue to their history and back ground. I want to know how religious they are. As Shakespeare's Hamlet intones "But that the dread of something after death, The undiscovered country, from where No traveler returns, puzzles the will".

I try to see if they still have any sense of humor left. If we can laugh, no matter how dark, there is a spark left.

My primary goal is to establish something that the person might be looking forwards to. It can even be as mundane as a favorite television show. I try to reinforce that "I understand that you want to kill yourself but why be in such a hurry. Let's meet first. We have established that we both (blank). You can always kill yourself any time, let's do this first."

I'm looking for a promise and the longer we talk the more likely I'll be able to get that promise.

If I get a hang-up I have a device that tells me where the call came from. My next call is to 911. Sirens and flashing lights tend to embarrass the neighborhood. Thankfully I've never had to use it.

Death is the one thing no matter how clumsy you are you will get right the first time. You really don't need practice sessions.

References
1 -- http://www.nimh.nih.gov/health/publications/suicide-in-the-us-statistics-and-prevention/index.shtml

2 -- http://www.vfw.org/News-and-Events/Articles/VFW-Stands-Up-Against-Military-Suicides/

3 -- http://www.msnbc.msn.com/id/44777299/ns/us_news-life/t/one-in-three-vets-say-iraq-afghan-wars-were-not-worth-it/#.T42bdNnv7Kg

---

Antidepressants and Suicide

How It Works With Non-SSRI Drugs
Suicide is a rare but known side effect of taking antidepressants. Since it is a rare side effect your doctor may tell you about it; then again, he may not.

Usually, suicide attempts occur after the patient has been taking the medication for awhile – several weeks or even months. Writers about antidepressants and suicide often conclude that since the suicide attempt happened after the medication had been taken for awhile the medication had obviously made the situation worse rather than better. This may well be the case with SSRI drugs, but with other types of antidepressants there is a different scenario.

Here is what actually happens when a person on other than SSRI antidepressants tries to commit suicide.

The person may have been thinking about killing themselves off and on for years. They may even have thought about several different ways of doing it. Those thoughts generally are most active during periods of depression where there is also an abundance of self-deprecating negative self-talk: "I'm not good enough." "I'm ugly. Nobody could ever love me." "Nobody wants me here. I should just go away." "I'm a horrible person." "I don't deserve to live." etc.

During periods of depression – especially deep depression – one's energy level is extremely low. It's hard to wake up; hard to get out of bed; hard to take a shower or get dressed or fix your own food or go to the grocery store or go to work or take a walk or do absolutely anything that requires the expenditure of energy. It is decidedly easier to let their minds wander or watch television or just sit on the sofa and smoke cigarettes. Doing stuff – anything – just takes too much effort!

Depressed people often don't shower, do sleep in their clothing, and don't socialize. They tend to prefer isolation.

Obviously, the suicidal thoughts are still there . . . maybe even the desire and the means are available. But – and it's a very big 'but' – there's no energy to put such plans into action. Therefore, no suicide attempts during this phase of one's illness.

Enter the antidepressants.

Antidepressant medications are not magic pills. It takes time for them to start lifting a person's mood. Generally, it takes about 4 weeks before they start having any effect. From there it could take much longer for the depression to lift. And during this time it's very likely that the suicidal individual will continue to think about – and possibly even plan – killing themselves.

Let me stress that NOT all depressed people consider suicide to be a viable option for their situations. Some people are suicidal; others are not. Some people can take antidepressants and not try to commit suicide.

When the depression lifts, this is the most critical time for the person because they can feel a burst of energy. It's like a dam broke and now the water comes rushing through. It can feel like exhilaration or awareness or just a feeling of normalness again. But their thought processes are still screwed up. The thoughts are still irrational. The thoughts are still about suicide and negative self-talk.

The thoughts are screwed up but the energy is now available to put these screwed up thoughts into action. And continuing to take the antidepressant continues to increase the available energy.

This is a very delicate situation because discontinuing antidepressant drugs compounds the difficulties these people find themselves in – especially if the drugs happen to be SSRIs (selected serotonin reuptake inhibitors). With SSRIs, the recommendation is "to withdraw extremely slowly from these drugs, usually over a year or more, under the supervision of a qualified specialist. Withdrawal is sometimes more severe than the original symptoms or problems."[1]

Discontinuing non-SSRI antidepressants may not be that difficult but any change in antidepressant dosage should always be under the supervision of your doctor. Never change the dosage on your own.

Anyway, the time between the antidepressant's lifting the depression and when the thought processes stabilize and become more normal is when suicide attempts are most likely.

There are 11 attempted suicides for every successful one. So what happens to these people who tried and were unsuccessful?

Initially they are taken to a regular hospital and given appropriate treatments to revive them. From there, when they are well enough, they are admitted into a mental health facility where they are examined (sometimes strip-searched to make sure they're not bringing in drugs or other contraband like matches or cigarette lighters) and placed on a locked ward where their street clothes are taken away and they're issued two hospital gowns – one to face backwards, the other to face forwards. Then they may have to sleep on a bed in the corridor for several nights under the watchful eyes of attendants (called suicide watch) while being fed psychotropic medications (very powerful stuff!).

References

1. – http://ssristories.com/

Suicide In The Elderly

Problems Of Aging, Statistics, And A Meaningful Life
By guest author: John F. Walsh, M.S.

"Grow old along with me! The best is yet to be"

That's all well and good but when you get up and its hard to walk without supporting yourself you kinda wonder, "How old was the the fool who wrote those words? "

When you look back at who you were and what you could do then that you can't do now it can get kind of discouraging.

The children are grown and have moved on except when they drop back with a load of laundry to get done. Then there are neighbors who have lost their spouse, have a chronic illness or just feel useless. In the minds of some is the feeling "why should I keep on?"

Some don't.

The National Institute of Mental Health reports there is one elderly suicide every 97 minutes. There are about 14.9 elderly suicides each day, resulting in 5,421 suicides among those 65 and older.

Elderly white men are at the highest risk with a rate of approximately 31.1 suicides per 100,000 each year. White men over the age of 85, who are labeled "old-old", were at the greatest risk of all; the suicide rate for these men was 45.42 per 100,000. That is 2.5 times the current rate for men of all ages (18.3 per 100,000). 84.4% of elderly suicides are male; the rate of male suicides in late life is 7.3 times greater than for female suicides.

The death of one is a tragedy . . . . the death of many? . . . just a statistic.

Consider Dave, diagnosed with A.L.S. He first noted a weakness in his right hand that spread to his legs. A few months later it progressed. He experienced a generalized clumsiness, stiff walking with overwhelming fatigue. It was then he felt panic as he felt difficulty swallowing or breathing, with muscle cramps during the night. He took stock of his future. Pretty soon he will not be able to care for himself. The burden will fall on his wife and whatever insurance he has left.

He has a long discussion with his wife. She doesn't like it but will accept her husband's decision. He fills the tub with hot water and with his wife holding his hand he kills himself.

Had I been on call I would be honor bound to rescue him. What exactly would I be rescuing him from?

Let's look at the flip side of this coin, another story, this one with less gloom and doom. It has to do with Mary. She was living in a retirement home and was very popular with the other residents -- some of it due in part to her notoriety, She was a can can dancer during the Alaskan gold rush of 1898. Her observation on her life? She said "No one really regrets the journey one takes. It was those who feared taking that journey that regretted their inaction."

There is a line in Meredith Willson's "The Music Man" that underscores Mary's observation; "If you wait for too many tomorrows all you will have is a handful of empty yesterdays".

That, my readers, is a significant clue to a satisfying life.
There is a place in Florida called Century Village. It was the brain
child of comedian/actor Red Buttons. It was creatively laid out with
apartment buildings, duplexes, family homes; structures familiar to
the the types of homes its occupants were familiar with how they
used to live.

Every week they brought in acts or groups to entertain the residents;
a Yiddish comedian for the city folks or square dancing for the
suburban crowds.

As a consultant to United Way's Retired Senior Volunteer Program
(RSVP). I got into a conversation with one of their residents. He
made an astute observation. He said, "I'm really grateful for what
they do for us. I just wish, someday they would ask something from
us."

The purpose of RSVP is to draw upon the talents of seniors who
volunteer to help others And that is another important clue to a
fulfilling life and a means for combating depression.

Get out of your house and get out of your problems and devote part
of your day to helping others.

Second, watch what you eat. Our diet usually consists of too much
fat, too much meat, too much salt, too many calories, and too much
fast food. Not only do we eat the wrong kinds of food, but we also
eat far too much at mealtime.

You have to begin sometime so make today the day you begin a
healthier life.

Third get off your butt and engage in age appropriate exercise. That
doesn't mean entering the local Tough Man contest or being a
participant in the Boston Marathon. It does mean attending to
movement, balance, blood pressure and breathing.

Third be an active participant in your own health needs. Sometimes doctors prescribe medicine to treat a certain condition not realizing that as you grow older that what you are taking can contribute to over-medication.

As you grow past retirement you might want to consider a physician who specializes in geriatric medicine.

According to Gail Sullivan, a professor at the UConn School of Medicine and associate director for education at the Center on Aging. fewer than 1 percent of all physicians in the country are certified in geriatric medication and treatment.

What are the common symptoms of elderly patients who are over-medicated?

• Fatigue
• Motor problems such as walking and standing
• Skin flushing and rashes
• Weight loss or gain
• Falling and problems with balance
• Mood swings
• Changes in personal hygiene
• Physical impairment
• Memory problems
• Hallucinations both visual and auditory
• Confusion
• Thinking and reasoning problems
• Abdominal pain
. . . symptoms that are easily confused with other psychiatric diagnosis.

Finally, get involved with your world. In the last presidential election, nationally at least 79 % of those 65 and older cast ballots. This is compared to an overall voter turnout of 52 percent, according to the U.S. Census Bureau.

You're retired so you have time. Learn about the different candidates in your town and on the national stage and keep in mind the different issues that affect your life and that of your family.

You are not just voting for one man, the president, Rather you are voting for a group of men and women who will be taking over the country and making decisions in your best interest – or, unfortunately, in their best interest. Be wary of bumper sticker solutions or "swift boating" a candidate's character or abilities. Whether you win or lose it will help you to be aware of the world around you, how it works and how it effects the quality of your life.

I complain that the years fly past, but then I look in a mirror and see that very few of them actually got past. ~Robert Brault

We are always the same age inside. ~Gertrude Stein

Bullying and Depression

Bullying in Adolesence, School Shootings, Teen Suicide
By guest author: John F. Walsh, M.S.

The world of an adolescent can be a minefield of insecurities. As a child you feel nurture. As an adult you experience autonomy.

As a teen you have one foot in the boat and the other on the dock. There is a strong need to belong which can lead to bad choices.

Your body is experiencing eruptions of your complexion and your emotions. It can be a time in your life when you feel lost, doubting your future and your abilities to shape that future.

If your body shapes to the smaller or weaker or you're just different in belief or social status, you may become a target to the bullying of others seeking to assert their imagined superiority.

Like a cur struck too many times you may seek to escape life altogether.

And with weapons so easily available you may decide to seek your own imagined superiority if just for a brief moment as you take vengeance against any and all who cross your path. Then you have another Columbine massacre.

Parents -- and even private citizens with no link to a child -- can help prevent school shootings, says Peter Langman, a psychologist and the author of Why Kids Kill: Inside the Minds of School Shooters (Palgrave Macmillan). Here are some of his suggestions:

-- "Set limits on your child's privacy. Keep open communication. Know your child's friends, what he does, what websites he visits. If there is a preoccupation with weapons or violent scenarios in journals, he may need help from a counselor."

-- "Pay attention to school warnings. If the school contacts you with concerns about your child's violent stories or class presentations, he may be depressed or enraged and need help. These 'red flags' have been noticed by teachers before school shootings, but parents rebuffed school officials."

-- "Eliminate easy access to guns at home."

-- "Recognize possible rehearsals of attacks. Some school shooters have done drawings, animations and videos or written stories in advance that depicted brutal acts."

-- "Stay alert to possible signs of future trouble. Private citizens have foiled rampage killings by youths. Among them: a clerk in a photo shop who noticed photos of a teenager with an arsenal of guns and someone who found a notebook with plans for a high school."

Suicide is the third-leading cause of death for 15- to 24-year-olds, according to the Centers for Disease Control and Prevention (CDC), after accidents and homicide. It's also thought that at least 25 attempts are made for every completed teen suicide.

Here is the case of Bobby Smith who lived in South Carolina (real person fake name).

Dan, Bobby's father, is a surgeon who specializes in gastric bypass surgery.

Gastric bypass surgery is the procedure that makes the stomach smaller and allows food to bypass part of the small intestine.

Dan feels that his sons should never settle for second place which presents a bit of a conflict because he has two sons.

Bobby's brother Mike is a year older and is first born and a natural athlete -- which makes it difficult to measure up to.

When Bobby entered the drama club (he had a beautiful singing voice) his father made a snide remark about a bunch of queers and insisted that Bobby try out for a a man's sport. Dan was a varsity halfback but had to drop out because of low grades. He was determined that his sons not share his embarrassment.

Bobby has trouble sleeping and is plagued with irritable bowel syndrome that appears resistant to treatment. Dan has a habit of joking about his sons to his friends -- usually when they are with him. To Dan, it's just affectionate pride. Bobby has trouble seeing the humor in Dan's remarks and cringes whenever Dan starts to introduce his sons.

Midterm exams come and Bobby scores a 79 out of 100. He leaves the ceremony and goes to his bedroom. An hour later he takes the family car.

Police say he must have been going in excess of 90 miles an hour when he hit a bridge abutment.

There was an overflow crowd attending Dan's son's funeral.

Depression and the Famous

Actors, Politicians, Writers. No One's Immune.
By guest author: John F. Walsh, M.S.

Feeling a little depressed or for that matter do you feel an emptiness? . . . like depression is overwhelming you? Alone in a prison of your own making? It's a lonely world isn't it? Actually you have a lot of company. Maybe, just maybe it may be a sign of creativity.

You have probably heard of Winston Churchill and his depression which he called his "Black Dog." You may have even heard that Newsman Mike Wallace almost committed suicide. It was during a time where he was sued by General Westmoreland for a story Mike did on the Vietnam war. BTW Mike was proven to be accurate.

There are others you might not have guessed. Let me share some of their stories.

How about Rodney Dangerfield, you know the comedian, " "I don't get no respect!," "No respect, no respect at all... that's the story of my life" Not his real name by the way it's Jacob Cohen.

He began to perform at the age of 20 under the name Jack Roy. Tried it for nine years without success. He tried his luck as a singing waiter until he was fired, and also working as a performing acrobatic diver before giving up show business to take a job selling aluminum siding to support his wife and family. That would depress anyone. The name Rodney Dangerfield was a fictitious character from the old Jack Benny show. And like Benny he developed a character who was the perpetual loser. When asked his real name he insisted it was Percival Sweetwater.

Actress Catherine Zeta-Jones checked into a Connecticut mental health facility to be treated for bipolar II disorder, which is characterized by swings between depression and hypomania.

The actress Gwyneth Paltrow revealed the post-postpartum depression she experienced in a 2008 interview with Vogue.

J.K. Rowling the creator of Harry Potter living as a single mother in a cramped apartment after separating from her first husband, J.K. Rowling suffered from suicidal thoughts and underwent cognitive behavioral therapy. She claims that the Dementors (the dark hooded creatures in "Harry Potter and The Prisoner Of Azkaban" who detect their victims' secret fears and then suck out their personalities) were based on her experience with depression.

Project Runway's Tim Gunn is the epitome of style. As a 17-year-old struggling with his sexuality, Gunn took more than 100 pills in a suicide attempt.

In a recent video for The Trevor Project, a national organization that aims to prevent crisis and suicide among gay and lesbian youth, Gunn explained, "I'm very happy today that that attempt was unsuccessful, but at the time it's all that I could contemplate."

He said he wants everyone who's feeling hopeless to know that "it gets better; it really does."

Peanuts creator Charles Schulz poured his depression into his comics, making Charlie Brown a sort of Everyman. After his death in 2000, Time quoted a friend saying, "I think that one of the things that afforded [him] his greatness was his unwillingness to turn his back on the pain."

Schulz took refuge in his comic strip and hoped it would give readers that same escape from their own everyday struggles.

One of the happiest seeming celebrity would be Ellen DeGeneres. The media frenzy caused by Ellen coming out in 1997 caused her to be mired in depression for three years. The controversy also reportedly put pressure on her relationship with then-girlfriend, Anne Heche, as well as contributed to the cancellation of her sitcom, Ellen. Rebounding with a vengeance, the talk show queen, now 52, currently is enjoying the success of a lifetime and is happily married to her longtime girlfriend, Portia de Rossi.

When you chose an alternative lifestyle you are going to bump into critics of your choices and their rejection and scorn is going to hurt.

As a performer your very livelihood is dependent upon the approval of the general public. Doubts of one's own abilities when it is those abilities that sustain your survival open the door to depression and self loathing.

As a psychologist I'm familiar with some of the histories I've reported. As for the rest a couple of evening curled up with Google opens the door to other discoveries. You would be surprised how many truly great people live lives of quiet desperation. I could go on but so can you. Look up the lives of:

Charles Dickens
Fyodor Dostoyevsky
Tchaikovsky
Abraham Lincoln
Edgar Allan Poe
Boris Yeltsin

Hans Christian Andersen
Astronaut Buzz Aldrin
William Faulkner
Ernest Hemingway
Hamid Karzai (President of Afghanistan)
Richard Nixon
Sir Isaac Newton
John D Rockefeller
Oprah Winfrey

These actors, artists, world leaders and authors were able to accomplish great things despite their struggles with the disease.

If they can, so can you.

Trapped in the prison of your own depression what goes on in the lives of others is irrelevant to your own sorrows. Yet they left the dark woods and and entered the clearing. It is said the depression is anger turned inwards.

When you feel down maybe this saying bares constant repeating; "I may not be much but I'm all that I've got so let me treat myself with the same respect that I afford others." (That's only fair isn't it?)

Try it.

Natural Treatments for Depression

Treatments for Mild Depression

Depression affects your mood, and can lead to major problems such as social withdrawal, sleeplessness, and even loss of appetite. Low levels of energy attributed to depression can cause you loss and lack of concentration, thus affecting your performance at work. Natural treatments for depression tend to perform best on mild depressive states. For more seriously debilitating conditions, medical intervention is advisable and the help of a qualified professional (counselor – psychologist – psychiatrist) is recommended.

There are many factors that can lead to depression. The first step towards treating depression is identifying the depressant. However, it is very easy to regulate your mood naturally. Everyone has the capacity to remain happy by keeping the happiness hormones active. These happiness hormones are serotonin (keeps you feeling good during the day) and Melatonin (lets you sleep soundly at night).

There are other natural healing processes that also help you cure depression naturally. The following are some of the most effective natural treatments.

Herbal Supplements
There are various herbs that help relieve symptoms of depression. Here are some of them:

Folate controls the functioning of the happiness hormone, and its deficiency leads to a low mood and depression.

SAMe (a.k.a. S-adenosylmethionine) is a herb that is rich in the antioxidants required for the healing of the CNS thus relieving depression.

Omega 3 fats are essential for proper coordination in the brain, thus relieving the symptoms of depression.

St. John's Wort (a.k.a. Hyperricum perforatum) is another herb that is believed to improve the functioning of the central nervous system.

Meditation and yoga
These are major techniques of relaxation. When you focus your brain towards an activity, your coordination rapidly improves. You forget all the troubles you are experiencing and subsequently overcome all the depressants in your life. Meditation and yoga have been used as natural treatments for depression for ages an can help heal all types of depression, as long as you concentrate.

Massage
Massage improved the circulation of blood, thus supplying all of your body parts with sufficient blood. Doing a massage on the head is especially helpful for the brain. This is because depression interferes with the normal flow of blood, and any effort to improve the circulation process produces healing effects.

Diet
Foods that are rich in magnesium, Vitamin B12, D, and fatty acids have a way of calming the brain. A balanced diet can prevent the development of any depression or flat moods. This is because your mood is determined by the foods you take.

Vitamins are vital for the natural healing, and boosting the functioning of brain cells. Magnesium has been found to relieve the symptoms of depression too. Other minerals are also essential, as they work together to ensure the smooth functioning of your body cells. This will protect you from the fatigue, weakness, and insomnia al of which are attributed to depression. The Mediterranean diet is especially good for people who are suffering from depression because it contains all the necessary elements required for natural healing therapy.

Some components in your beverages could worsen your condition. Sometimes people turn to caffeine, alcohol and other hard drinks in order to self-medicate their depressive feelings. This only makes the condition worse. Avoid caffeine and alcohol and instead drink a lot of water. Water will help keep your body hydrated and protect you from migraines associated with dehydration.

Music therapy and exercise is also used to counter the impacts of depression.

Counseling
Some depressants are hard to deal with, especially those that cause chronic depression. Situational depression -- when you lose a loved one either through death, separation or divorce – may trigger extreme grief which may necessitate seeking the help of a professional. And some experiences may leave you depressed never to heal.

Normally, mild depression should lift on its own within a few weeks. However, if you are taking too long to heal, it is time to make an appointment with a counselor, psychologist, or psychiatrist. If you have tried all natural therapies but the hurting feelings are still fresh in your mind, talk to a professional. They will offer a therapy to help you recover. Sharing your problems is one of the most effective strategies for confronting tough times. Therefore, you can even try sharing with a trusted friend.

Resources
Mayo clinic: Depression (major depression)
URL:
http://www.mayoclinic.com/health/depression/DS00175/DSECTIO
N=alternative-medicine

WebMD: Alternative Treatment for Depression
URL: http://www.webmd.com/depression/guide/alternative-
therapies-depression

Livestrong: Foods that heal depression
URL: http://www.livestrong.com/article/69221-foods-heal-
depression/

NCBI: Rapid recovery from major depression using magnesium
treatment
URL: http://www.ncbi.nlm.nih.gov/pubmed/16542786

Your Happy Hormones
http://www.drrossdc.com/happy%20hormone.htm

Herbs For Depression

Depression can be a symptom of a psychological or physical
problem. Either way, prescription drugs can leave one with side
effects like dry mouth, sleepiness or a feeling of being detached from
reality. Using herbs for depression seldom leaves your body with
any negative effects when dosage is taken as recommended.

According to many medical researchers, s-adenosyl-L-methionine is a chemical that is produced in the body. When this substance is lacking, different types of depression can kick in. The good news is that several herbs are known to stimulate this chemical's production, bringing your s-adenosyl-L-methionine levels back to where they belong.

Here are a few herbs that have been studied and found to be effective for relieving certain depressed states.

Ginkgo Biloba

Ginkgo Biloba, a.k.a. Maidenhair Tree, grows in two small areas of Eastern China and is currently being cultivated in Korea and Japan. They are said to be able to live at least 1,000 years and some as long as 2,500 years or more and are very useful as food and herbal medication.

An extract of the leaves of Ginkgo Biloba is popularly known as an herb that enhances memory and concentration but it has several other qualities including the relief of asthma and wheezing, anti-allergenic and anti-inflammatory capabilities, aids in treating senile dementia, deactivates free radicals indicated in cancer causation and Alzhiemer's disease, and helps with impotence and erectile dysfunction.

This tree has been delivering medicinal value for thousands of years. It is believed that the flavonoids and terpenoids found within the leaves of the Ginkgo Biloba tree are the active ingredients that provide a variety of healing properties. Especially useful for treating depression in the elderly, these ingredients work together to protect and expand the blood vessels. This small function alone can improve blood flow to the brain, helping to enhance memory but also to create an uplifted spirit.

Dosage

"The recommended usual dosage for Ginkgo Biloba, standardised to 24% ginkgoflavonglycosides, is 40mg three times a day – morning, afternoon and evening. It is important to have constant, steady blood levels of circulating Ginkgo Biloba in the blood at all times." For those not responding well to other antidepressant medications, 80 mg 3 times a day provided significant improvements in mood, motivation and memory with four weeks of starting treatment.

Caution:
"Do not take more than the recommended dose.
Toxic reactions may result if taken in excess.
People on anti-clotting drugs should not take ginkgo."

Rhodiola Rosea -- (a.k.a. Golden Root)
Another ancient plant is said to have improved the strength and endurance of warriors in Siberia, where the plant originated. Also called Golden Root, the Chinese have used Rhodiola Rosea tea leaves for eliminating fatigue, decreasing depression and stimulating the nervous system. Hypertension, sleep disorders and irritability have also shown marked improvement with use of these natural plant leaves.

"Doses used are commonly 200 to 600 mg/day. For depression, doses of 340 to 680 mg/day of R. rosea extract (as SHR-5) have been evaluated for up to 12 weeks."

American Skullcap
There are two distinct herbs called Skullcap: American Skullcap and Chinese Skullcap. They are not interchangeable. Neither is recommended for children.

The American Skullcap plant is a member of the mint family, is native to America but is now cultivated in Asia and neighboring Russia. Many natural and healing properties can be found in this small plant found deep in wooded areas. Some of these include Tannins, Catalpol, Scutellarin and bitter iridoids.

Native American Indians have long used Skullcap for the following nervous disorders:

* Epilepsy
* Hysteria
* Anxiety
* Drug Withdrawal
* Depression
* Insomnia

Be careful when purchasing Skullcap as, in the past, it has been grown with Germander, a plant that damages the liver. Make sure you're buying from a reliable dealer. Do not exceed the recommended dosage and do not use at all if pregnant or breastfeeding.

Living with depression can leave one very secluded from the rest of the world and drugs often have to be changed, monitored and leave unfavorable reactions. The above herbs have been studied extensively and have been shown to be effective. However, always check with your physician prior to taking herbal remedies to make sure there will be no adverse interactions with whatever pharmaceutical medicines you're current taking.

For mild depressions, treating depression naturally seems sensible in keeping your body functioning properly.

References
http://treatingdepressionhelp.com/homeopathic-remedies-for-depression
http://www.herbsfordepressionrelief.com/gingko-biloba.html
http://www.herbwisdom.com/herb-rhodiola.html
http://www.drugs.com/npp/rhodiola-rosea.html
http://www.umm.edu/altmed/articles/skullcap-000273.htm

Medical Treatments for Depression

Headache Remedies

Pharmaceutical and Natural

CAUTION: Headache remedies presented here are for educational purposes only and are not intended to diagnose or take the place of consultation with a qualified health care provider. See your doctor if your head pain is unusually severe or if it lasts longer than a day or two. Also, if you notice that your headache is caused by some new stimulus, i.e. a new trigger. Other symptoms indicating the need for emergency professional intervention are headache with:
-- vision changes
-- problems with movement
-- confusion
-- seizure
-- fever
-- stiff neck

According to a report by Dr. Robert Smith, published in the 1997 issue of Hospital Medicine, headaches are the primary cause of 10 million doctor visits per year.3 More than 45 million Americans are plagued by recurring headaches and of those, 28 million – or about half – are migraine headaches.4 Recurring pain can be a cause of depression.

Since headaches are an extremely common complaint and since many people don't like the side effects associated with pharmaceutical remedies for getting rid of recurring pain, people have devised many effective medical and non-medicinal ways of finding relief.

Headache Medicines – (pharmaceutical)
Some of the most popular over-the-counter medicines for relieving headaches are aspirin, Tylenol (acetaminophen), Advil (ibuprofen), and Aleve (naproxen). Though all are effective at relieving most headache pain, for those with frequent and recurring bouts of pounding head pain frequent use of these medicines should be avoided. Rebound headaches – headaches that return as soon as the medication wears off – are a serious consequence of medication overuse.

An overdose of acetaminophen can be toxic. Recommendations say, "No more than 2 (pills) in a six hour period!"[5] However, extended use of low doses of this medication can also be toxic.

There are also specialized medications for specific types of headache, i.e. 20+ popular brands for migraines alone. Imitrex and sumatriptan are said to be very helpful for relieving this type of pain.

Some doctors recommend lithium medication[1] as one of several pharmaceutical headache remedies for severe migraines and other headache types caused by tension or sinus involvement. The symptoms can include severe head pain, nausea, vomiting, and light and noise sensitivity. While lithium carbonate might well ease the immediate pain, it has the potential for creating long-term problems whereby "the cure could be worse than the disease".
(Read about potentially life-altering lithium side effects in the section on lithium.)

Before going down that path, why not explore the potentially equally effective but less potentially harmful ways to find relief without medication? As one astute blog commenter put it, "Why take drugs if you can solve the problem naturally?"

Natural Headache Remedies
For best relief, different types of headaches require different types of treatment (see next section for symptoms). For example, many headaches are caused by stress. Here are some suggestions for relieving stress or tension headaches:
-- a neck massage to loosen the neck muscles
-- physically leaving the stressful situation . . . go for a walk outside
-- changing your posture . . . sit up straight instead of hunched over your desk
-- do relaxation exercises
-- take a warm bath . . . add some pleasant aromatics to the water
-- take a warm shower . . . let the spray massage your scalp
-- place an ice pack on your temple, forehead, or the back of your neck

Consider these suggestions for relieving a migraine:
-- eliminate light and noise . . . cover your eyes or sit or lay in a very dark quite room
-- take a nap
-- eliminate any unnecessary movement . . . especially of your head
-- if your migraine is caused by perfume, go away from the smells

Cluster headaches are rare, affecting less than 1% of adults, but if you're affected you want relief. Try these:
-- oxygen therapy . . . breathing oxygen from a canister at higher concentration than air. Do not breathe pure oxygen as that can cause blindness.
-- get checked for sleep apnea . . . 80% of cluster headache sufferers also have sleep apnea. Fix one and you may fix the other.

Sinus headache sufferers may find relief by:
-- holding warm packs against the painful area
-- using a humidifier or vaporizer

-- using a saline solution nasal spray
-- trying nasal irrigation to flush mucus out of the nasal passage
-- avoid irritants such as cigarette smoke, perfume, or various chemicals that irritate nasal passageways

There are also herbs for treating headache pain, chiropractic treatments that make neck and spine adjustments that are said to bring effective and lasting relief, and a myriad of other non-medicinal interventions. You can find many of these alternatives by searching the Internet. Just use common sense when considering their use.

4 Main Headache Types
Headaches and headache symptoms are classified under 4 main categories.2 Knowing the type of headache you experience will help you treat it more effectively.

1. Tension
a. Episodic Tension Headaches (experienced LESS than 15 days per month)
-- constant pressure or throbbing mild to moderate pain
-- pain affects any part of the head . . . top, sides, front
-- short duration (30 minutes) to several days
b. Chronic Tension Headaches (experienced MORE than 15 days per month)
-- almost constant pain throughout the day . . . intensity may vary
-- pain can affect any part of the head . . . top, sides, front
-- pain waxes and wanes over a long time
Associated symptoms include
-- waking up with head pain
-- sleep disturbance, i.e. difficulty getting to sleep or staying asleep
-- chronic fatigue, i.e. always tired
-- difficulty concentrating
-- mildly sensitive to light or noise
-- general muscle aches

2. Migraine

Migraines have varied symptoms that may or may not include pain. The classic migraine includes having no pain but seeing bright flashing lights, blind spots, an aura of wavy or jagged lines, or, in my case, an irregularly shaped yellow to orange donut outlined in black that undulates and moves as the color becomes bright white and the center of the donut disappears. Its duration is no more than about 30 minutes but during that time I'm unable to read because of a blind spot caused by the flickering lights.

Other migraine symptoms that can occur in various combinations include:
-- moderate to severe throbbing pain affecting the whole head or moving from one side of the head to the other
-- sensitivity to light, noise or odors
-- blurred vision
-- nausea, vomiting, upset stomach, abdominal pain
-- loss of appetite
-- feeling very hot or very cold
-- loss of skin color, i.e. paleness
-- fatigue
-- dizziness
-- fever (rare)

3. Cluster
-- intense burning, throbbing or constant pain on one side of the head
-- pain in the eye region or stationary behind one eye and not changing sides
-- duration varies, 15 minutes to 3 hours (usually 30 minutes to 90 minutes) and usually one to three headaches per day
-- regular occurrence at the same time each day and may awaken the individual at the same time each night

4. Sinus
-- deep constant pain that affects the front of your face . . . cheekbones, forehead, bridge of the nose
-- sudden movements make the pain worse
-- usually in conjunction with other sinus symptoms, i.e. runny nose, fever, facial swelling, ear problems

References
1. -- http://www.webmd.com/vitamins-supplements/ingredientmono-1065-LITHIUM.aspx?activeIngredientId=1065&activeIngredientName=LITHIUM
2. -- http://www.webmd.com/migraines-headaches/guide/migraines-headaches-symptoms
3. -- http://www.vegfamily.com/lauren-feder/tip1.htm
4. -- http://abcnews.go.com/Health/Wellness/headache-relief-best-home-remedies/story
5. -- http://www.wikihow.com/Get-Rid-of-a-Headache#Natural_remedies

Postpartum Depression Treatments

PPD Depression and Treatment

Giving birth is supposed to be one of the happiest moments in a woman's life but sometimes it isn't. Postpartum depression refers to a condition in which a new mom has a severe depression after giving birth. This reaction can manifest even six or more months after the baby is born. In such cases, it is important for a qualified professional such as a counselor, psychologist or psychiatrist to identify which postpartum depression treatments may be most effective for helping the mother cope.

Postpartum depression can leave you feeling anxious, restless, lonely and fatigued. Mood swings and self-loathing are common symptoms of this condition. Feelings of anger at having one's life totally disrupted and restricted because of the new responsibilities may be directed towards the baby. These feelings are not uncommon – sometimes accompanied with thoughts of wanting to harm the child. If this is the case, separating the mother and child for a time may be necessary.

It is believed that hormonal changes during pregnancy that quickly subside after giving birth can play a large role in causing postpartum depression. If you have the above listed symptoms, you should consult your doctor. She can provide a referral to an appropriate professional.

Counseling and therapy – sometimes in conjunction with proper medication -- can be an effective postpartum depression treatment. Below is a list of other effective treatments.

Antidepressants:
The almost thirty kinds of antidepressants that could be prescribed for postpartum depression relief are classified into four main types. They are:
-- Tricyclics
-- MAOIs (Monoamine oxidase inhibitors)
-- SSRIs (Selective Serotonin Reuptake Inhibitors)
-- SNRIs (Serotonin and Noradrenaline Reuptake Inhibitors)
-- NASSAs (Noradrenaline and Specific Serotoninergic Antidepressants)
It's believed that they increase the activity of brain chemical neurotransmitters which are the chemicals involved in transmitting signals from one cell to another.

Most doctors will recommend one or another of the above for treatment of postpartum depression. However, it is important to note that some are not safe when you are breastfeeding because they can pass into the breast milk and harm the child. It is therefore important to inform your doctor that you are breastfeeding before taking any antidepressant so he can prescribe the appropriate medications for your case.

An important consideration in taking antidepressants is the risk of suicide (which is a known, though rare, side effect). Talk with your doctor as soon as you start feeling better. He may want you to stop taking the medication.

Cognitive Behavioral Therapy:
Going for professional counseling can help you overcome your anxiety and depression. The role of a counselor is to help you find better ways to think about your new life situations so you can deal with them in a more effective manner. The therapist can also help you set realistic goals and work with you to ensure that you achieve them.

For therapy to be most effective, however, it helps to have the support and love of your family. This is because research has shown that mothers that receive support and help from older women about how to care for a baby feel more confident and are less likely to experience postpartum depression. Having someone who's "been there – done that" giving you advice goes a long way towards relieving anxiety and instilling feelings of "I can do this!"

Hormone therapy:

Since hormone imbalance, caused by a dramatic drop in progesterone following the birth of the baby, plays an important role in this condition, your doctor may recommend hormone replacement therapy. This involves a replacement of either progesterone or estrogen as determined by a blood test so as to counteract the body's no longer making high levels of that substance. However, this therapy, just like other pharmaceutical medications has its side effects and it is important to work with your physician so he can help you weigh the pros and cons. Sometimes antidepressants are prescribed in conjunction with hormone therapy for maximum results.

ECT -- a.k.a. Electro Convulsive Therapy:
Electroconvulsive therapy (ECT) is sometimes used in extreme cases to help control the symptoms of PPD. With this procedure, a small amount of current is applied to your brain. The remedy is usually used when other treatments have failed. It has been shown to be effective in reducing symptoms.

Other Remedies for Postpartum Depression
Alternative remedies for postpartum depression such as herbal remedies have been shown to work wonders. Some herbs that can be used include St. John Wart herbs, oat straw, Siberian Ginseng, Ginkgo Biloba, basil, clove, passion flower and valerian root. The best thing about treating postpartum depression with herbs is that there are no side effects. It is also cost-effective.

Resources:

http://www.mayoclinic.com/health/postpartum-depression/DS00546/DSECTION=treatments-and-drugs
http://www.nlm.nih.gov/medlineplus/postpartumdepression.html
http://www.nlm.nih.gov/medlineplus/postpartumdepression.html
http://www.rcpsych.ac.uk/mentalhealthinfoforall/problems/depression/antidepressants.aspx
http://www.livestrong.com/article/108551-medications-used-treat-postpartum-depression/

Celexa And Pregnancy

Is Celexa Safe To Use While Pregnant or Breastfeeding?

So, to answer the question, "Do Celexa and pregnancy go together?" – the answer is a qualified, "It depends." Not a very definitive answer, but you'll understand better as you read through the rest of this article.

Celexa is a very powerful selective serotonin reuptake inhibitor (SSRI) used to treat major depression. It can provide certain undeniable benefits, but it also comes with some very known and disturbing shortcomings. Pregnancy adds another level of complication to the decision. Specifically, what effect Celexa will have on the developing fetus.

There are three different classifications of antidepressant medications that have been approved by the FDA for use during pregnancy. Celexa is one of them. This doesn't mean that there are no potential risks of birth defects for the baby. It just means that the risk of birth defects and other postnatal problems for the infant are very low.

There are also risks for the mother if she decides to not take antidepressant medication while pregnant. Some of those risks include a very low energy level which could lead to not taking good care of herself, or not eating the kinds of foods the baby needs to become healthy, or not seeking good prenatal care, or even trying to self-medicate with cigarettes and alcohol (which could also cause birth defects). All of these would have deleterious effects on the developing fetus which could result in premature birth and/or low birth weight and other postnatal problems.

The decision of whether to take antidepressant drugs while pregnant or not is best made by the doctor and patient discussing the pros and cons together – weighing the benefits and the risks to each -- to reach a decision that would be best for both mother and child. The very low incidence of birth defects associated with the use of Celexa include a serious lung problem in newborns called persistent pulmonary hypertension of the newborn (PPHN) when the antidepressant was used during the last 4 months of pregnancy as well as heart defects associated with the tissue that separates the two ventricles. There is also the possibility of other rare birth anomalies such as human spontaneous abortion or other complications requiring prolonged hospitalization arising immediately upon delivery.

Fetuses exposed to Celexa after the third trimester may experience neonatal withdrawal syndrome upon birth. This includes irritability, constant crying, shivering, eating and sleeping difficulties and convulsions.

Celexa and Breastfeeding
Breastfeeding is NOT recommended for new mothers who are taking Celexa. Celexa, a.k.a. citalopram, passes into breast milk. Breastfed babies receiving Celexa tend to experience a decreased desire to feed and weight loss.

The antidepressant manufacturer recommends discontinuation of either the antidepressant or the breastfeeding.

Discontinuation of the medication could pose serious problems for the mother. Withdrawal is a long, slow, drawn-out process that can take over a year to complete. You can read more about SSRI withdrawal symptoms in the next section.

Celexa and Weight Gain
Usually, Celexa acts as an appetite suppressant which results in weight loss while on the medication. However, about 1% of patients report a weight gain. If you're in this group, consult your health care provider. You may need a different antidepressant or some counseling in making various lifestyle changes – eating healthier foods, exercising more, limiting alcohol consumption.

Rapid weight gain is more often seen in people who have gone through withdrawal and are no longer taking the drug. This is a known and described result of stopping this medication.

References

http://www.mayoclinic.com/health/antidepressants/DN00007
http://www.webmd.com/baby/news/20030714/taking-ssris-in-pregnancy-affects-infant
http://www.drugs.com/pregnancy/citalopram.html
http://www.obfocus.com/reference/Formulary/Drugs%20in%20Pregnancy/Citalopram.htm

SSRI Medications

Selective Serotonin Reuptake Inhibitors

WARNING: "Antidepressants increased the risk compared to placebo of suicidal thinking and behavior (suicidality) in children, adolescents, and young adults in short-term studies of major depressive disorder (MDD) and other psychiatric disorders."1

Click Here for the SSRI FDA Warning, revised on 3-28-2012, for people with heart problems.

SSRI List with their most popular U.S. Brand Names (not inclusive)
-- citalopram hydrobromide . . . . . . Celexa, Cipramil
-- escitalopram oxalate . . . . Lexapro
-- fluoxetine . . . . Prozac
-- fluvoxamine maleate . . . . Luvox
-- paroxetine . . . . Paxil
-- sertraline . . . . Zoloft
-- dapoxetine . . . . Priligy
-- mirtazapine . . . . .Remeron
-- clomipramine . . . . Anafranil

History
Prozac was the first SSRI to be introduced in 1987. At that time, less than 1% of the American population was diagnosed as Bipolar. That percentage has grown. Now over 4.4%, or 1 out of every 23 people in the U.S. has been diagnosed with bipolar disorder (a.k.a. manic depression).

Uses
All of the above are prescription medications that were originally used to treat major depression. Over the years their off-label uses have grown and are increasingly prescribed to treat: eating disorders (they act as an appetite suppressant), alcoholism, premenstrual dysphoric disorder PMDD), social anxiety, PPD (postpartum depression), headaches, panic disorders, OCD (obsessive compulsive disorder), PTSD (post traumatic stress disorder), and other conditions.

Effects

The theory is that depression is causes by a "brain chemical imbalance" among the neurotransmitters (a description promoted as a marketing hook by pharmaceutical companies) – or a lack of serotonin in the brain. Since the SSRIs inhibit the dissolution of this neurotransmitter by the nerve cells, once serotonin is secreted it remains and its level increases causing an elevation in mood.

The effect of antidepressant drugs on the brain has been likened to that of LSD.

This theory does not take into account the fact that the majority of serotonin (more than 90%) is metabolized elsewhere in the body, not just in the brain. Its regulatory functions include the endocrine system as well as the smooth muscles of the digestive system (which may account for its actions as an appetite suppressant). Inhibiting its ability to be reabsorbed in the brain also inhibits its reuptake in the rest of the body as well – causing possible complications for those organs.

SSRI Side Effects

Many of the physical side effects of SSRIs tend to be temporary and mild. These include: insomnia, rashes, headache, joint and muscle pain, stomach upset including nausea and diarrhea. If they occur at all, they usually go away within a few days to a few weeks.

SSRIs affect the blood's ability to clot. Internal bleeding within the stomach or intestines can be a serious problem, especially if the patient is also taking NSAEDs (aspirin, Tylenol (ibuprofen), Aleve (naproxen), or COX-2 inhibitors).

Sexual functioning may be diminished with SSRI use. For men taking Viagra, lowering the SSRI dose or switching to a different antidepressant may help.

SSRI use doubles the risk of suicidal thinking -- especially in children and adolescents, but also in adults. There is also the risk of inciting violent and/or self-destructive actions.

Withdrawal
The fact that a very lengthy, professionally supervised withdrawal period of over a year is needed in order to discontinue use should raise some red flags. Withdrawal is associated with addiction or dependency and "can cause severe neuropsychiatric and physical symptoms. . . . Withdrawal can often be more dangerous than continuing on a medication . . . (and) is sometimes more severe than the original symptoms or problems."2

Adverse Reactions
The critical times to be most watchful for adverse reactions are:
1 – when starting or discontinuing any of the SSRIs
2 – when increasing or lowering the dose
3 – when switching from one SSRI to a different SSRI

Adverse reactions are often diagnosed as bipolar disorder even though they were entirely treatment induced. Over 200,000 Americans per year are hospitalized with antidepressant-associated mania and/or psychosis.2

Other adverse reactions could include: bizarre behavior, school shootings or other school incidents, road rage, arson, postpartum depression, murder or attempted murder, suicide or attempted suicide, murder-suicide, workplace violence, air rage incidents. This is not an exhaustive list of possibilities.

Positive Reactions
Obviously, all the news about SSRIs is not bad because they continue to be prescribed and they continue, in some cases, to be very helpful in spite of their shortcomings.

The SSRIs make it possible for some people to continue functioning and contributing in meaningful ways to their families and society.

If considering the use of SSRI drugs, I would urge you to take an active role in the final decision. Discuss BOTH the pros and cons of these drugs with your health care provider. Before coming to a final decision, be fully aware of what you're getting into.

IN CASE OF EMERGENCY/OVERDOSE
Local poison control center **1-800-222-1222**
If victim has collapsed or is not breathing . . . . **call 911**

References

1. --
http://bipolar.about.com/od/antidepressants/a/antidepressant_1boxwarning.htm
2. – http://ssristories.com/
http://www.health.harvard.edu/press_releases/ssri_side_effects
http://www.medicinenet.com/citalopram/article.htm

What Is Lithium?

Here are the Sections of this article:
-- **What Is Lithium**
-- **What Is Lithium Used For**
-- **Lithium Medication**
-- **Lithium For Bipolar Disorder**
-- **Side Effects Of Lithium**
-- **What Is Kidney Disease**
-- **What Does Thyroid Disease Affect**

What Is Lithium

Lithium in its pure state is an extremely light (Li = 3 on the periodic table of elements) silvery-gray alkali metal that is highly reactive with water and/or air. The pure state can be artificially produced in a laboratory; it is never found that way in nature.

The natural state of lithium is as a compound – or salt. Named from the Greek "lithos" – meaning stone or rock -- lithium is commonly found as a metallic ore in igneous rocks or as a salt in mineral springs. It's believed to have been one of only three elements (hydrogen, helium, lithium) produced in quantity by the big bang. Lithium is known to be toxic for humans when taken internally in large amounts; smaller amounts are used as medication.

What Is Lithium Used For

One of the primary uses for lithium is as medication – specifically as a mood stabilizer for people with bipolar disorder. I'll discuss this use in more detail later in this article. Right now I'd like to touch on the many other uses for this metal.

Energy – Lithium-ion batteries have emerged as very efficient energy storage systems. They are used to power everything from battery operated toys to automobiles. The energizer bunny is a fitting symbol for its capacity; it just won't stop!

Industrial Uses – Lithium carbonate when combined with silica and other materials is used as a low-melting flux. A flux as used in welding helps to reduce oxidation and facilitate the melting and joining of metals under extremely high heat. It's also used in the manufacture of glass ovenware for baking. It is used in both low-fire and high-fire ceramic glazes, tile adhesives, in the processing of aluminum, and for carbon dioxide sensors. In closed-air spaces like aircraft and submarines, lithium can trap carbon dioxide, thereby acting like an air purifier.

Pyrotechnics – Colors are very important for pyrotechnic displays. When burned, lithium's color is either deep red or, under extremely high heat, bright white.

Lithium Medication -- As early as 1843, lithium carbonate was being used as medication to dissolve stones in the bladder. Other ailments included "gout, urinary calculi (calcium deposits in the urinary tract), rheumatism, mania, depression, and headache."1 In 1970, the FDA (Food and Drug Administration) approved its use in the treatment of mania for those with bipolar disorder (a.k.a. manic depression). More recently, lithium has been found to be effective in delaying the progression of amyotrophic lateral sclerosis (ALS). Lithium applied topically has been used to treat dermatological conditions such as herpes viral infections. This is just a partial list of its many medicinal uses.

WARNING: Do not take lithium if you are pregnant, planning to become pregnant, or breastfeeding. It is harmful to a developing fetus. It can also pass into your milk and harm your infant.

WARNING: Do not give lithium to children younger than 12 years of age.

Lithium for Bipolar Disorder

Lithium carbonate is used to lower the mania – or intensity -- of manic episodes in those experiencing bipolar disorder (a.k.a. manic depression). How it does this is not known, but the theory is that it may work by increasing the activity of the brain's chemical messengers. "Lithium affects the flow of sodium through nerve and muscle cells in the body. Sodium affects excitation or mania."2

Here are the signs of manic behavior:
-- hyperactivity
-- talking fast
-- poor judgment
-- needs very little sleep
-- aggression

-- anger
It's not necessary for all of these to be present at the same time for behavior to be seen as manic.

The benefits of using lithium to control mania include:
-- a reduction of symptoms
-- shorter mental hospital stays (usual stay about 2 weeks)
-- prevention of future manic episodes
-- provides the possibility of living a more productive life

However, ingestion of lithium also has its drawbacks, namely . . .

Lithium Side Effects

Lithium carbonate and lithium citrate are considered safe for use and have been approved for human ingestion by the US Food and Drug Administration (FDA). The safety of lithium orotate is questionable at this time and avoidance is recommended until its safety can be confirmed.

Some side effects are immediate and temporary; others are permanent.

Lithium can cause allergic reactions. Get emergency medical treatment if you experience any of the following: "hives; difficulty breathing; swelling of your face, lips, tongue, or throat."

Call your doctor if you experience any of these serious side effects:
-- extreme thirst or excessive urination
-- weakness, restlessness, confusion, eye pain or vision problems
-- restless muscle movements in your eyes, tongue, jaw or neck
-- pain, cold feeling, or discoloration in fingers or toes
-- light-headed, fainting, slowed heart rate
-- hallucinations, blackouts, convulsions (seizure)
-- fever with muscle stiffness, sweating, fast or uneven heartbeats
-- lithium toxicity (nausea, vomiting, diarrhea, drowsiness, muscle weakness, tremor, lack of coordination, blurred vision, ringing in your ears)

Less serious immediate side effects may include:
-- mild hand tremor
-- weakness or lack o coordination
-- mild nausea, vomiting, loss of appetite, stomach pain or upset
-- thinning or drying of the hair
-- itching skin

(The above partial list of immediate and temporary lithium side effects information came from drugs.com/lithium.html)

Two of the permanent side effects of lithium ingestion are (or can be):
1 – kidney disease
2 – thyroid disease

What Is Kidney Disease

Kidney disease is a silent killer that affects every organ of the body! In chronic renal failure (CRF), over a long period of time (could be over 30 or 40 years) the kidneys lose their ability to remove wastes from the bloodstream. The disease symptoms are "silent" – meaning you don't know that anything is going wrong – until the kidney nephron (filtration) malfunction reaches approximately 75% and toxic wastes begin to accumulate in the bloodstream.

As toxic wastes increase, anemia increases and energy levels plummet. Everyday tasks become increasingly difficult simply because of the lowered energy levels. Urine output increases including increased nighttime urination which further reduces energy because of interrupted sleep time.

End stage renal failure (ESRF) occurs when approximately 90% of the nephrons have been destroyed and the filtration rate is down to around 10%. Options at this point include dialysis, transplant, or death.

The end stage renal disease process (ESRD) can be slowed down by adopting certain life-style changes such as stopping smoking, eating a healthier diet, and/or taking certain medicines, but there is no treatment that will reverse the damage or halt the progression of the disease once it has begun.3

(Read more about the timeline for chronic renal disease in the next section.)

What Does Thyroid Disease Affect

"The thyroid is a small gland in the neck, just under the Adam's apple. Shaped like a butterfly, the thyroid plays an important role in a person's health and affects every organ, tissue, and cell in the body.

It makes hormones that help to regulate the body's metabolism (how the body uses and stores energy from foods eaten) and organ functions. When the thyroid is not working properly (called thyroid disorder), it can affect your body weight, energy level, muscle strength, skin health, menstrual cycle (periods), memory, heart rate, and cholesterol level."4

Lithium damage to the thyroid gland produces an underactive thyroid condition known as hypothyroidism. This condition can be regulated by taking daily medication for the rest of your life.

References

1 – http://en.wikipedia.org/wiki/Lithium_carbonate
2 – http://www.drugs.com/lithium.html
3 -- Miller, Martha J. Kidney Disorders. Medical disorders and their treatment. Encyclopedia of Health. New York: Chelsea House Publishers. c. 1992.
4 -- http://thyroid.about.com/cs/addisonsdisease/a/overview.htm

http://www.nami.org/Template.cfm?Section=About_Medications&Template=/TaggedPage/TaggedPageDisplay.cfm&TPLID=51&ContentID=20820

http://www.wisegeek.com/what-is-lithium.htm

Chronic Renal Disease

Timeline of Physical Changes in Chronic Renal Disease
Since kidney disease can be one of the permanent side effects of ingesting lithium, and since once kidney disease begins it inevitably progresses to the point of kidney failure, and since it is 'silent' -- meaning you don't know that damage is occurring until the latter stages of the illness -- it may be important to look at the physical changes that occur within the body as this progression is taking place.

First, we'll look at the symptoms of acute renal failure (ARF) which happens relatively quickly.

Next, we'll innumerate the physical changes over time as chronic renal disease (CRD) becomes chronic renal failure (CRF).

Symptoms of Renal Failure

Acute Renal Failure (ARF)

The kidneys suddenly stop working.
Urine output is less than one (1) pint per day.
a. Metabolic waste products, acids, and potassium accumulate in the bloodstream.
(excessive potassium = irregular heartbeat = heart failure)

b. Fluid and sodium retention may cause edema of the face and extremities, high blood pressure, accumulation of fluid in the heart and lungs = heart failure from fluid overload.

Foods to avoid: milk, cheese, nuts and peas because these contain large amounts of phosphorous. Avoidance is necessary because the kidneys are unable to eliminate the excess.

Foods to limit: meat, nuts, milk, fruits and vegetables because these contain potassium which can also reach unhealthy levels.

Complications: the most frequent complication in ARF is infection. (infection = death if not controlled)

Stages of Chronic Renal Failure (CRF):

Stages I - IV
The kidneys over a long period of time (could be 30 - 40 years) lose their ability to remove wastes from the bloodstream.

Symptoms are "silent" until nephron malfunction reaches approximately 75%.
At which time:
a. paradoxically, urine output increases (polyuria) because water and sodium are not being properly reabsorbed from the damaged kidneys.
b. glomerular filtration is at a fraction of its normal level
c. toxic wastes are beginning to accumulate in the bloodstream

(kidney disorders = more water consumed = even higher urine production – including increased nighttime urination which interferes with sleep time = decreased energy)

Stage V
End Stage Renal Failure -- ESRF
a. ± 90% of the nephrons are destroyed
b. ± 10% glomerular filtration rate

One's choices at this stage are:
1. dialysis
2. transplant
3. death!

Symptoms of ESRFare:
1. anemia = pale and weak
2. increase in uric acid levels
"When these levels rise, uric acid crystals may be deposited in joints and soft tissues, leading to gout." Miller, Kidney Disorders, p. 81.
3. skin color changes = waxy, yellowish color of skin tone
Extremely high urea concentration may result in fine white urea crystals on the surface of the skin.
4. poor appetite = loss of weight
5. nausea = loss of weight
6. vomiting = loss of weight
7. urine-like odor of the breath
8. open soars that bleed severely may form in the stomach and intestines
9. skeletal changes
a. release of calcium from the bones = weakened skeleton and possible depositing of calcium in soft tissue throughout the body. This is most dangerous when occurring in the heart, kidneys, and/or lungs.
10. nervous system changes (in later stages)
a. poor concentration
b. fatigue
c. weakness
d. restlessness
e. insomnia
f. slower nerve impulse conduction
g. burning pain, numbness and tingling of the feet and toes. This may progress up the leg.
and, eventually -----
h. convulsions
i. coma
j. progressively falling blood pressure, then

k. rapidly falling blood pressure, then – within hours
l. DEATH !

Treatment for Chronic Renal Disease

The disease process can be slowed down by adopting certain life-style changes such as stopping smoking, eating a healthier diet, and/or taking certain medicines, but there is no treatment that will reverse the damage or halt the progression of the disease once it has begun.

References

Miller, Martha J. Kidney Disorders. Medical disorders and their treatment. Encyclopedia of Health. New York: Chelsea House Publishers. c. 1992.

History of Kidney Disease

From 400 B.C. to 1992 A.D.
Since kidney disease can be one of the permanent side effects of lithium medication, I thought it might be interesting to look at how the current treatments for this disease evolved.

This timeline was compiled over the course of a year or two from my extensive reading for my own curiosity so the references never got recorded. I tried to make it as accurate as possible but am making no promises.

History of Kidney Disease

Date Event

? 400 B.C. Hippocrates (ca.460 - ca.377 B.C.), a Greek physician and the Father of Medicine, was the first to document certain symptoms and relate them to a dysfunction of the kidneys. Some of these symptoms were:
(1) blood or puss in the urine indicated infection
(2) bubbles on the surface were associated with kidney failure
(3) the sudden appearance of blood was linked to hemorrhage
(4) sandy sediment meant the possibility of kidney stones

2nd Century A.D. "(T)he Greek physician Galen (129-ca. 199) thought that there were sieves inside the kidney that helped filter out impurities and waste products from the bloodstream into the urine. This idea, which essentially was not far from the truth, persisted for many centuries." Miller, Kidney Diseases, p. 16.

800's Doctors studied the works of Isaac Judaeus, a medieval practitioner who analyzed urine (including color, odor, and sediment) for diagnostic purposes.

1500's Urine analysis, aka urinalysis, was widely overused to diagnose kidney disease even though the resulting diagnoses were often dangerously inaccurate. The College of Royal Physicians in London denounced treatments based solely on diagnoses made by urinalysis to the exclusion of other techniques.

? 1550 A.D. Andreas Vesalius (1514 - 1564), a well-known artist of the time, made drawings of kidney structure, and there had been some progress in understanding its disease. However, until about 100 years ago (1900) little was known about its function.

1659 Marcello Malpighi (1628 - 1694) discovered the existence of "little balls" within the kidney. This discovery was not well received by his colleagues who dismissed this new information and vehemently defended their outmoded "Galen's sieve" model of kidney function.

prior to

1700's "Blood, pus, sediment, protein, and sugar were all studied and associated in some way with disease." Miller, Kidney Disorders, p. 18.

These are all substances which appear abnormally in the urine. Question: What kind of sugar (refined? natural and present in unprocessed foods?) was studied and associated with disease? Or, can't tell once it's in the body!? And does it make a difference? Some say, "No." I say, "Yes." but this is for the next chapter. Is sugar in the urine associated with kidney disease, or simply 'disease' as in diabetes?

? 1700's Frederick Deckers (1648 - 1720) discovered that heating certain urine samples would cause coagulation which is associated with protein in the urine. Diseases such as nephritis (inflammation of the kidney) or nephrosis (a disorder characterized by retention of fluid in the body) are associated with protein in the urine.

1770's Urea, the waste product produced when the body uses protein, was identified. "Urea is the primary waste normally eliminated by the kidneys. When kidney function fails, urea cannot be eliminated sufficiently, and when it accumulates in the bloodstream, a life-threatening condition called uremia develops." Miller, Kidney Disorders, p. 18.

1842 Following the development of the microscope (first developed between 1590 and 1610 by Hans, father, and Zacharias Janssen, son. A more powerful microscope was developed around 1673 by Anton Van Leeuwenhoek with subsequent improvements over the intervening years.), "Sir William Bowman (1816 - 1892), a British physician, reexamined Malpighi's work and found it to be basically sound. Bowman, however, went one step further and identified one of the central mechanisms involved in urine formation – the process of filtration." Miller, Kidney Disorders, p. 18.

mid 1800's The beginnings of working out the theories and methods for dialysis, i.e. filtering the blood through a selectively permeable membrane outside of the body. The earliest theories were put forth by Thomas Graham (1805 - 1869), a Scottish chemist.

late 1800's The workings of the kidney were just beginning to be understood. Prior to this date, "(b)ecause of this lack of knowledge, kidney diseases, although frequently noted, were typically misunderstood and inadequately treated." Miller, Kidney Disorders, p. 15.

1913 Dialysis on animals was first attempted by John Abel at John's Hopkins University. The blood's tendency to clot in the external tubes was a major problem.

1917 during WW I. "A. R. Cushny, a Scottish professor, elaborated upon the reabsorption mechanism associated with urine production. Through this mechanism, substances that have filtered into the nephron (the small structural unit in the kidney that acts as a filter for the urine) – but are still needed by the body – are absorbed back into the bloodstream instead of being eliminated." Miller, Kidney Disorders, p. 19.

1945 the end of WW II. A crude prototype of a 'kidney machine' for use with people had been developed.

1967 a new law allowing people to give permission while they are alive for the donation of all their organs following death by signing a 'uniform donor card'
Without the signed card, doctors can approach the grieving relatives of a brain-dead potential donor. Even with the signed card, I believe the relatives can still say no.

1982 ethical concerns surfaced concerning the limited supply of donor organs

Who gets them? wealthy people who can afford to pay for the operation? equally disabled persons, but needing financial assistance to pay for the operation? people who know how to mount an advertising campaign?
Can a living person sell an organ to the highest bidder?
What about organ thieves? If there is a profit to be made, someone will find a way.
1990 9,800 kidney transplants were performed in the U.S.

The groundwork for transplants was laid as early as 300 B.C. with skin grafts that were performed in India. These surgical techniques were brought to Europe in the 16th century by traders where they were promptly condemned by the Catholic church as "interfering with the will of God". With the advent of anesthetics to kill the pain and antibiotics to fight infection and tiny needles so necessary for such delicate surgery and tissue typing and the development of anti-rejection drugs in the 19th and 20th centuries, transplant success became more realistic. And research is still continuing to make the odds even greater.

1992 Dialysis is a necessary and common treatment for people with kidney disorders.

Depression Services

Where Can I Get Help For Depression

-- 24 hour HOTLINES AND HELPLINES

National Hopeline Network --- **1-800-784-2433 (1-800-SUICIDE)**
http://www.hopeline.com/

National Suicide Prevention Helpline --- **1-800-273-8255 (1-800-273-TALK)**

Other Depression Helplines
http://www.dbsalliance.org/site/PageServer?pagename=crisis_hotlin
einfo

How To Help Someone With Depression

Editor's Note: Friends and family can be very helpful for someone experiencing the lows of a depression but in order for them to know HOW to help I asked our guest author and experienced psychologist of 45 years to give us a few tips.

How To Help Someone With Depression
By guest author: John F. Walsh, M.S.

When a psychiatrist views the dis-ease of depression they frequently link it with anxiety as if it were the same illness. Tagging along behind is an emotion called "worry". Let's herd them into separate pens and give them a closer look before we brand them.

First let's examine the critter called "worry" Under a cold hard stare we can strip it of its outer covering and see it for what it is. Worry is nothing more and nothing less than negative fantasy.. A fantasy of everything that could go wrong will go wrong. Worry in the short term can be helpful "Did I leave the water running?". To satisfy this worry you check to see if the faucets are turned off and you go on with your life. But for some worry is an addiction. The person becomes so consumed with worry that it freezes the will from any decisive action.

A close side running partner to worry is "anxiety". What's the difference between the two? With worry you are mentally stuck in the past. With anxiety you are mentally stuck in the future. Let me give an example.

You are facing a big chemistry mid term. exam You are anxious that you won't do well, that you haven't studied hard enough, and even if you did What would a failing grade do to your other subjects.

So you take the exam and lo and behold you flopped it, big time. Now you are no longer anxious you're sad and worried. You don't feel anxious about the test now you just feel regret that it happened the way it did. Suddenly you feel anxious again. Will you flunk out of college? What will your parents say? Will you have to go to work? What kind of job will you be able to get?

Regrets of the past can lead to anxiety of the future.
By now you are probably aware of the difference between situational depression, (you flunked out of school and feel sad about it) as opposed to Clinical depression you feel profoundly sad without any obvious reason. Things may be going well for you but this dark wave of sadness washes over you....and stays.

A doctor would explain that the patient's level of serotonin was too low. Serotonin is primarily found in the gastrointestinal (GI) tract, platelets, and in the central nervous system (CNS) of animals including the gastroenteritis of humans. It is popularly thought to be a contributor to feelings of well-being and happiness.

Which only goes to show you really need guts to overcome depression.

So you would like to help someone who is depressed.

First you need to take a reading of whether your friend even wants your involvement. You can let your friend know that if he or she wants to vent that you will be there for them. Wait a heartbeat or two to see if the slats open. if it doesn't you have shown your willingness to help.

If your friend does vent then listen, understand but do not pass judgment. And for heaven sake keep your slats closed; don't you start venting. It should not be a contest of "Nobody knows the trouble I've seen." -- *and don't try to fix it with unsolicited advice* like ""Have you tried aromatherapy? There was an article about it in the paper…" . This kind of comment can come across as trivializing your friend's concerns. Just let your friend know you are on their side and let him have his say.

Be there but also realize your friend has arrived with a monkey on their back. When they leave the monkey goes with them.

While it is important to accept the person in the state they are in, don't let it totally consume your life. Otherwise, you'll fall in a heap and won't be much help to anyone. You need to take care of yourself. "I am committed to you and to helping you. But I also need to eat / shop / go out for coffee / ring a friend / see a movie to recharge my batteries. Then I can look after you better."

"We don't see things the way they are. We see them the way WE are." -- Talmud.

"The reason people find it so hard to be happy is that they always see the past better than it was, the present worse than it is, and the future less resolved than it will be." – Marcel Pagnol

# # #

Many of the articles (case studies) in this book were written by my friend, John (Jack) F. Walsh, M.S. If you found them useful – or simply enjoyed them – and would like to read more of Jack's thoughts, please consider checking out his book:

Clinical Psychology – A Professional Perspective – memoirs and experiences

Disclaimer

Information presented on this website and forum is intended for educational purposes only and is not intended to substitute for or take the place of advice from a qualified medical professional. Nothing here should be viewed as an individual medical recommendation.

Any use of the information by you is SOLELY AND COMPLETELY AT YOUR OWN RISK AND RESPONSIBILITY. We take no responsibility for your actions.

For individual medical advice, consult your personal health care provider.

About the Authors

Joyce Zborower, M.A. earned her Master of Arts degree in clinical psychology from Bradley University. Her post-graduate work included college level courses in anatomy, physiology, and nutrition as well as considerable independent study.

She also trained as a jewelry designer with Bob and Gina Winston at their studio in Tempe, Az., and has had her original step-by-step jewelry designs published in various international magazines such as LAPIDARY JOURNAL, JEWELRY ARTIST, WIRE JEWELRY, just to name a few.

More recently, Joyce has been writing and publishing books and special reports on the Amazon kindle platform and on Google Books. Click here to visit her page at Amazon.com

Jack F. Walsh, M.S.
1937 - 2012

Following two years working for the Daytona, Fla Police Department Jack Walsh received his master in clinical psychology from Bradley University.

While taking a master class in Rorschach (ink blot test) taught by Samuel Beck, one of the three top names in Rorschach interpretation, he was invited to attend the University of Chicago PhD program. He elected, instead to spend at least one year in every phase of mental health treatment available. This includes a 7000 bed hospital outside of Chicago, a center for special needs children in North Carolina, Director of a Model Cities program in Charlotte, N.C., forensics training in Columbia, SC leading to his certification as non medical forensic examiner for the state of South Carolina, just to name a few.

Jack is an award winning photographer whose photo essay on the Chicago riots was featured by The Business Executives Against the Vietnamese War. He continued sending photographs of conflicts from Chicago, Prague, East and West Berlin, Belfast and Londonderry. He has currently authored his first book, Clinical Psychology – A Professional Perspective – memoirs and experiences, which covers forty five years of our history as seen from a satirical eye. It is available from Amazon.

One Last Thing Before You Go. . .

Thank you for purchasing *Different Types of Depression.* If you enjoyed it or found it useful, would you take a few moments and write a short review on its Amazon page? Also, please let your friends know about it on Facebook and Twitter. If it makes a difference in their lives, they will thank you. As will I.

All the best
Joyce Zborower

Amazon Top 3 Bestsellers in Depression

(1-12-2014)

1.

Mindfulness: An Eight-Week Plan for F...
by Mark Williams
4.6 out of 5 stars   (85)
Kindle Edition

$8.63

2.

Feeling Good: The New Mood Therapy
by David D. Burns M.D.
4.4 out of 5 stars   (558)
Kindle Edition
$4.74

3.

An Unquiet Mind: A Memoir of Moods an...
by Kay Redfield Jamison
4.3 out of 5 stars   (602)
Kindle Edition
$9.99

Digital Books by Joyce Zborower

Click here to go to my Amazon page
-- MYSTERIES/SHORT STORIES
The Trust – a cautionary tale

Little Mysteries – a short story

-- CRAFTS BOOKS

Handcrafted Jewelry Step by Step – 6 intermediate and advanced original designs

Handcrafted Jewelry Photo Gallery – cast jewelry -- fabricated jewelry

Wire Jewelry Photo Gallery – Original designs

Creations in Wood Photo Gallery – jewelry boxes, screens, storage ideas

Bargello Quilts Photo Gallery – quilt wall hangings

Bargello Train Quilt – cutting and sewing instructions

Sell Your Work – how to turn your craft into your business

-- FOOD/NUTRITION RELATED BOOKS

No Work Vegetable Gardening – for in-ground, raised, or container gardening

How to Eat Healthy – foods to eat . . . foods to avoid

The Truth About Olive Oil – benefits, curing methods, remedies

External Uses of Extra Virgin Olive Oil – Folk Remedies ... Body Lotions ... Pet Treatments

Signs of Vitamin B12 Deficiencies – Who's at Risk – Why – What Can Be Done

13 Easy Tomato Recipes – nature's lycopene rich superfood for heart health and cancer protection

3 Fruit Pie Recipes – apple, cherry, crisp persimmon

BBQ Spare Ribs Recipe – with homemade honey BBQ sauce

-- PSYCHOLOGY BOOKS

Psychology of Success – how to have success when trying to change how you look

Different Types of Depression – Characteristics and Treatments

How to Fight Depression – 9 case studies ---- by John F. Walsh

Clinical Psychology – A Professional Perspective – memoirs and experiences – John F. Walsh

-- CHILDREN'S BOOKS

Christmas ABCs – cute animal illustrations

Baby Pics Counting and Number Book -- 1-13 The numbers are in numerals and words with lots of photos of babies.

Most of the above are also available as print-on-demand paperback editions. Also:

Grandma's No Work Vegetable Gardening – (paperback edition) same as *No Work Vegetable Gardening* except the photos are B&W and the price is lower.

Español Libros (Spanish language Books)

Haga click aquí para ir a mi página de Amazon -- http://amzn.to/MlKKpJ

Pequeños Misterios – cuento

Joyas Artesanales Galeria de fotos – Joyas fundidas – joyas forjadas

Joyas de Alambre - Galería de fotos – Diseños originales

Creaciones en Madera- Galería de fotos – joyeros, biombos, ideas de almacenaje

Quilts Estilo Bargello - Galería de fotos – tapices de quilt

Quilt Tren en Bargello – instrucciones para cortar y coser

Vende tuTrabajo – como transformar tu arte en negocio

Signos de deficiencia de vitamina B12 -- Quén esta en riesgo – Por qué - Qué puede hacerse

Huerto sin Esfuerzo – para jardinería en el suelo, elevada o en contenedor

La Verdad Acerca del Aceite de Oliva – beneficios, métodos de curación, remedios

3 Recetas de Pie de Fruta -- Manzana, Cereza, Caqui fresco

13 Recetas de Tomate Fáciles -- Superalimentos de la naturaleza ricos en licopeno para la salud del corazón y protección contra el cáncer

Receta de Chuletas de Cerdo en Barbacoa -- con salsa casera de barbacoa con miel

Fotos de Bebés Libro de Números y de Contar De 2 a 5 años – 1 – 13

ABCs de Navidad – Para niños de 2 a 5 años

Italian Language Books

La verita su olio de oliva ... Prestazoini – Metodi di polimerizzazione -- Rimidi

Other Recommended Books

Ab Workouts for Hardgainers ---- by Michael Weston

Basic Ab Workouts Give You Sexy Flat Abs --- Michael Weston

The Confession of a Trust Magnate ----- by George Allen Yuille

> *Picture the combined navies of the world anchored off our seaboard cities, the combined armies of the world in possession of our inland cities, envoys from each nation congregated at Washington partitioning our country, the entire population being apportioned as slaves to do the bidding of the conquerors.*
> *Would you be interested?*
> *An equally appalling situation confronts the people of this country to-day.*
> *Read of it in the pages of this book.*

This book was written in 1911. Its message is critical for today – 2014.

Printed in Germany
by Amazon Distribution
GmbH, Leipzig

31045387R00061